T0339689

The Remote Work Handbook

The Remote Work Handbook: The Definitive Guide for Operationalizing Remote Work as a Competitive Business Strategy is for readers seeking to leverage the business benefits of a flexible, remote workforce. It is a practical guide for building and implementing remote work at any size organization. C-suite executives, operation leaders, business owners, or entrepreneurs who recognize the workplace is changing can use it to re-tool their operations for a strategic business advantage. Mari Anne Snow, the author, is a recognized remote work expert with over 20 years of experience leading remote teams and has re-written the rules of leadership to unlock the potential in remote and distributed teams. In this book, she shares all her secrets.

The book explores the untapped potential of remote teams and lays out the business case for adopting a new, flexible workplace model to build organizational resilience and a competitive edge. It takes the reader through the step-by-step process of constructing a remote work operating model, staging an implementation, then institutionalizing and sustaining the change. It includes down-to-earth professional and personal stories that alert the reader to alert the reader to the top priorities and operational realities they will face as they craft their own implementation plan for operationalizing remote work at their company.

The Remote Work Handbook

The Definitive Guide for Operationalizing Remote Work as a Competitive Business Strategy

Mari Anne Snow

Routledge
Taylor & Francis Group

A PRODUCTIVITY PRESS BOOK

First published 2023
by Routledge
605 Third Avenue, New York, NY 10158

and by Routledge
4 Park Square, Milton Park, Abingdon, Oxon, OX14 4RN

Routledge is an imprint of the Taylor & Francis Group, an informa business

ISBN: 978-1-032-15307-0 (hbk)
ISBN: 978-1-032-15305-6 (pbk)
ISBN: 978-1-003-24355-7 (ebk)

DOI: 10.4324/9781003243557

Typeset in Garamond
by KnowledgeWorks Global Ltd.

Dedication

In loving memory of Linda, my forever person, who stood
by me through thick and thin. I hear your voice in my heart.
Miss you every single day.

Contents

Acknowledgments

Thanks to the hundreds of remote professionals around the world who have shared their remote work stories with me over the years. To Cathy Z. and Brian W., two of the most skilled remote professionals ever. You taught me more than you'll ever know. To my husband, Charlie, who supports me without question – even when it takes attention away from him, poor guy. Thanks for being my best decision ever. To my international family, thanks for coming into my life and making it so rich and amazing. You are a great fan club. I am grateful for your continued love and support. To Rob H. and Alison J. who put me on the right path and gave me the confidence to complete this project. To my editor, Kris, for taking a chance on me, showing such patience and good humor. To Andrea T. for your unending friendship, support, and helpful feedback. To Amy F. and Adriana C. for endlessly formatting the manuscript for me. To Zim and Nancy for helping me transform my ideas into the great illustrations in this book. To my little sis, Karen S. who always lets me choose, and always respects and supports my choice. To David H., Adam C, and my many other geek buddies for your invaluable insights on infrastructure. I am very grateful to have all of you in my life.

About the Author

Mari Anne Snow, CEO of Sophaya and the Remote Nation Institute, successfully led remote/distributed teams for over 20 years. Early on, she sensed the growing strategic business implications of remote work as a global financial services executive where she launched an online corporate learning university that served 28,000 people in 32 countries. And as a professor at Bentley and Suffolk Universities during the early days of digital/social media, she helped position her students for success by helping them craft a place for themselves as the first digital professionals at Reebok, Nike, the New England Patriots, Fidelity Investments, and other notable organizations. Early on, she saw the strategic implications of these new technologies on remote/distributed teamwork.

A passionate businesswoman committed to people-centric leadership, Mari Anne recognized both the enormous potential of these emerging technologies to support remote work. She developed new leadership approaches to meet the needs of the people impacted by this seismic shift. Then she left corporate life in 2010 to launch her remote work/distributed team consultancy, Sophaya, to help visionary early adopters transform their organizations to accommodate the structural needs of their growing remote/distributed workforce.

Over the next 10 years, Mari Anne devoted herself to refining best practices for leading a productive, engaged remote workforce. During this time, she focused on two questions: 1. How do we maintain meaningful human contact over distance? 2. What actions can smart leaders take to build trust and engage people who work remotely? Her research spanned multiple continents, testing alternate operating models, and gathering input from hundreds of remote work practitioners worldwide. The results? A new set of business principles for creating highly productive remote teams to support the workplace revolution that's happening right now.

Introduction

This introduction provides the context, identities, and objectives for this handbook. It alerts readers that this is a practical implementation guide for anyone interested in creating and implementing an operating model that accommodates and supports a virtual, hybrid, dispersed, distributed, or remote workforce. The author points out that everything in this handbook is a proven, practical technique that the author has field tested and verified through years of experience and research as a successful senior executive and a dedicated remote work implementer. This introduction offers background on the history of remote work and highlights the current shifts happening in workplace culture. The author argues we need to re-write the rules of leadership and workplace etiquette as old, traditional approaches are ineffective or downright destructive in this new, flexible work environment. She alerts business leaders that early adopters who understand this is the future of work and who pivot now will reap the best business advantage and gain a competitive edge over their competitors who don't.

Virtual teams, hybrid teams, a dispersed, or distributed workforce, and employees working from home have a lot in common. They are all forms of remote work with distinct characteristics that require new business skills to achieve top productivity. These new business skills differ from in-person, traditional office operating models as they must support a workforce that gets work done in a virtual office rather than a physical one. Today it's easier than ever to create a virtual office structure as it is now possible to run many types of businesses without expensive office real estate. All you need is an open mind, a little creativity, internet connectivity, an eye toward cybersecurity, and the appropriate device. The year 2020 was THE definitive global Proof Of Concept (POC) that many, many more jobs can be performed outside a physical workspace than previously thought. The pandemic highlighted the business potential of the flexible work model and going back to the "old ways" means taking a step backwards. Why give up business gains when in 2020 a lot of the really hard change management work for you and the business world, along with today's workforce, are already more than halfway there?

Remote work isn't new, it's been around for a very long time. You may well have engaged in remote or distributed work for years without realizing it. If you used your laptop or tablet during business travel, checked work email from your smartphone, or participated in a conference call or video chat, congratulations, you've worked remotely. You've been part of the growing mobile workforce. Globalization, rapid technological advances, light-weight mobile devices, new software platforms, and the rise of cloud computing have provided the technical infrastructure that enables remote work. Ironically, the infrastructure changes provide remote workplace access and allow remote work to take place but the most important part of the equation, the people launched into this new way of working, are left scrambling to catch up. Managing, leading, and achieving remote work productivity and team engagement have gone woefully unaddressed. Remote professionals have been left to figure it out themselves as corporate learning departments, business schools, business executives, and many of our office-bound colleagues have failed to recognize remote work as legitimate. They continue to apply outmoded business practices to this new mobile workforce to the frustration of everyone involved.

This handbook aims to change that by presenting an alternate way of looking at remote work. In my experience, remote work is a largely untapped, strategic business tool available to anyone as a business differentiator that provides market advantage. There are lots of different ways organizations can apply remote, distributed, hybrid work strategically, and I'll discuss each of them in this handbook. If you are reading this, you, too, see the competitive advantage of decentralizing your operations, reducing your fixed-cost office footprint, and leveraging team productivity in more flexible ways. You recognize remote work and dispersed teams create resilient employees that can more easily adapt to change; encourage the development of a mature, independent-minded workforce, and expand your talent pool so you can build highly skilled distributed teams. You see the possibilities of approaching remote work as a novel, innovative business opportunity. You are a leader in the future of work, and you have come to the right place. This handbook is the step-by-step guide that outlines the necessary steps to intentionally re-tool your existing operating model or create a brand new one that supports a distributed workforce and flexible workplace options.

Everything in this book is a practical, proven best practice. In it, I share over 20 years of experience, research, and wisdom from my own remote work career as well as hundreds of hours of interviews with skilled remote professionals. This is a collection of the absolute best bits that will fast track your remote work implementation as you customize things to suit your unique business objectives. Happily, everything I discuss in this book is universally applicable to whichever remote work model you choose. I'll give you the basic framework. Then you can tweak your plan and build the systems that best support your business goals, company values, and operational needs.

Chapter 1

Workplace Flexibility Is a Smart Business Move

Testing Your Assumptions – What Is a Remote Team?

There is a lot of talk about remote work these days. But often there is confusion as to what remote work is and how prevalent it is in business today. Remote work presents itself in lots of different forms – remote, hybrid, digital nomad, hot-seating, virtual, distributed, dispersed, or work-from-home. There are lots of names for it and it's easy to get confused. For simplicity's sake, I've standardized the definition for this handbook. Going forward, when I refer to remote work, I'm talking about any worker or work team that has these three distinct characteristics:

1. Some or all of the team members are physically separated in some way and do not share the same physical workspace at the exact same time.
2. Team interactions, communication, collaboration, and work processes are supported by and dependent upon technology, both hardware and software, and are enabled by internet access.
3. Team members are real, live people, not automation, who must ignore physical distance and utilize technology to form effective working relationships, convey information, build team culture, and execute on their work obligations. [1]

DOI: 10.4324/9781003243557-1

Competitive Advantages of Remote Teams

I understand that not everyone is sold on the business benefits of remote work. Ironically, most remote work skeptics have unwittingly worked remotely for years. Anyone in business who worked while traveling, engaged in business phone calls, conference calls, or video meetings has already done it to some extent. It isn't a question of when remote work will come to business, it's already here, and no amount of skepticism will stop it now. From a practical perspective, it isn't feasible to assume that everything can be done in-person when technical advances provide such a cost-effective, time-efficient alternative. Remote work can't be ignored as a viable business strategy. There is a lot of data pointing to the competitive business advantages of remote work. In this handbook, I am offering a way to structure and organize remote work so you can use it to gain a business advantage and win against your competition. Some of the more obvious business benefits often cited in remote work research include:

- cost efficiencies with reduced overhead and more flexible, less fixed-cost workplace options.
- productivity gains from work efficiencies, greater team resilience, and less operational disruptions.
- less downtime due to pandemics, weather events, or other environmental disruptions.
- quality of life gains for employees, leading to more job satisfaction and reduced turnover.
- a reduced carbon footprint from reduced commutes and less business travel.
- a larger, global talent pool to draw from, particularly in fields that require specialized talent.

Here are a few others you may not have considered:

This Is an Opportunity to Access the Potential of Your Existing Remote Talent More Effectively

Traditional "home office" companies rarely leverage talented remote employees that work outside a company's central home office. Employees who work elsewhere are still part of your workforce and they are a significant untapped resource. Few leaders take the time to search for talent outside their immediate line of sight and companies fail to build meaningful career paths for remote professionals. Remote professionals rarely figure into succession planning or top talent discussions. Many existing managers have a natural prejudice toward them, viewing remote employees as slackers, if they think of them at all. I witnessed this myself on many occasions. In many of the large companies I worked for, it was common knowledge that "home office" employees had a built-in career advantage because they shared office space with company executives. Proximity provided visibility and opportunities to schmooze. Even when their work performance was subpar, visibility won. Meanwhile, the remote workforce scattered across the globe was rarely recognized for their achievements or tapped for choice assignments or promotion. They were not celebrated for their value or evaluated based on their business contribution. They were an under-appreciated resource often marginalized, forgotten, or dismissed.

I spoke with one highly skilled technology professional, Ryan, who told me about his experience as the only remote member of his team. Ryan was the chief technologist for his business unit with critical expertise in the company's IT systems. While he had lots of positive feedback from colleagues who worked with him often, his overall team experience told a different story. Ryan worked in a separate location from his team because of his role. He rarely had the time or budget funds to visit the home office and show his face. His boss and co-workers often neglected to include him in important communications regardless of how many times he reminded them. It was not unusual for him to be ignored on audio conference calls where he could hear his colleagues speaking about him like he wasn't there. Things finally came to a head one day when he called into the office to seek help with an issue only to discover his entire team was at a team retreat, an event he had no knowledge of, and for which he never received an invitation. He left the company shortly after this incident, taking his legacy knowledge and expertise with him to the competition.

Sadly, these experiences are not unique. Typically, remote workers have been considered of lower status and subjected to the suspicions of bosses and co-workers. Rather than feeling like a valued and trusted part of the company, these folks tend to rally around local regional leaders as that is the best path to advancement. They remain on the margins, disengaged and silent until something better comes along. This disconnect breeds a high degree of change resistance, team division, and adversarial relations in dispersed organizations. Regional loyalty trumps company loyalty, making wholesale company change almost impossible to achieve. Talent and company resources are needlessly wasted, productivity suffers, and team dynamics are constantly fractious.

Remote work business models level the playing field and offer a way to change this unhealthy dynamic by engaging remote employees in new and interesting ways. When a remote employee feels like a respected and trusted team member it's easier to unlock the remote employee's potential and maximize their business contribution. Companies that value and include remote employees gain the full value of every team member. When we treat remote employees as we treat office employees, it levels the playing field for all employees and raises the standard for everyone. There is more available talent within your full talent pool to help with the workload and people feel part of the team regardless of their work location.

We saw this happen in many companies in 2020 and 2021 when companies with remote employees adopted "camera-on" video conferencing as a team standard. Everyone felt a little awkward at first, but many remote employees indicated they felt seen and heard for the very first time. Remote team dynamics shifted positively as everyone shared the same virtual space. For the first time, it felt like everyone was equal. Team camaraderie blossomed and team rivalries resolved themselves. Folks pulled together because the work mattered more than the work location. Businesses that turned their backs on these employees by returning to old ways in 2021 and beyond experienced high rates of turnover as remote employees, discouraged by their loss of status, left to find other workplace options that recognized their remote work value. Whereas companies that embraced the remote work ethos and continued to acknowledge and include remote employees experienced higher retention rates and realized significant business gains.

Highly Skilled Remote Employees Add a Lot of Business Value and Need Less Managing

Successful remote professionals master the ability to work independently and self-direct their own work performance. The best ones are great problem solvers, critical thinkers, and assume responsibility for their actions. In short, they are self-accountable adults managing themselves. A well-managed remote workforce can function independently when expectations and deliverables are defined, technical access is fully enabled, infrastructure is provided, objective feedback is delivered, support is given, and information is shared. Remote employees are more resilient and much less averse to change. Once the operating infrastructure is in place and remote work business skills are taught, your remote teams will function self-sufficiently, and they can manage more complex tasks.

Remote workers still need the support of their managers, but the support they need is different. They need managers who can trust them, coach them, and advocate for them. What they don't need is control and policing. Remote professionals don't tolerate micromanagement. They are frustrated with poor or opaque communication practices and are rapidly disillusioned if they sense they are being ignored or disrespected. To get the best from your remote employees, it takes new leadership approaches to lead this type of workforce as the relationship between boss and team member is less hierarchical and more collaborative. We'll discuss this in greater detail in Chapter 7.

Retaining Valuable Remote Talent Is a Smart Cost-Savings Strategy

Remote work saves you money if it helps you retain experienced, valued existing employees. Losing a skilled employee is a costly blow to a company. If you are losing your best talent because they hate their commute or because they need to move because of a family circumstance, it's time to actively consider ways you can use flexible work options to get them to stay. I've known many experienced professionals going through unexpected life events who liked their jobs but felt they had no choice but to leave their companies because remote work was not an official option. These people worked for traditional employers skeptical of remote work. Even though many of these employees were well established in their careers and well respected, valued contributors, their bosses made no effort to retain them. I helped many of these employees build business cases for a remote work option and then coached them on how to negotiate with their employers to give remote work a try. Many of them succeeded and went on to long, prosperous careers with their companies as a result. In these cases, the employers incurred small out-of-pocket expenses that were more than offset by the productivity gains realized from a skilled, engaged employee.

These remote employees thought creatively and adapted to change quickly because they were already used to doing things differently. They often took the lead on new ideas because they had less fear of change. Plus, they understood how things worked in their companies and were well respected by their peers, so they could convince reluctant colleagues to try new things. These folks picked their living place in support of their interests rather than their jobs. One friend of mine told me, "I thought I hated my job, but after I went remote and gave up my 2+ hour commute I discovered I loved my work again." Happily, for everyone, his employer valued my friend's contributions so much they were willing to consider alternate work arrangements. This flexibility allowed my friend's employer to keep a trusted, knowledgeable team member and, as a result, my friend is now a rejuvenated employee because of the lifestyle change. This is also a smart, viable solution in tight labor markets when employers are fighting for talent and struggling to hire. Investing in retention helps stem the bleed and stabilizes operations. Offering flexible work options to existing staff is a compelling incentive for many employees struggling with burnout or quality of life issues. I've encouraged many of my clients to consider flexible work options as a cost-effective strategy for reducing employee turnover.

Remote work has broader application than you might realize. It isn't just a solution in the more obvious industries like tech and professional services. In 2021, I worked with one healthcare group that was about to lose a valued, experienced practice manager named Tara who oversaw operations at multiple healthcare clinics for the group. Tara's husband had received an excellent job offer out of state and the family was set to move. Meanwhile, the labor market was tight and there were few people applying for Tara's position. Candidates that did apply had less experience and were asking for substantially more money. Tara was beloved and capable. She had the trust of her team, her boss, and she was highly skilled at her job, so her employers didn't want to lose her. During 2020, much of her work happened remotely so there was an existing proof of concept that remote work was a realistic possibility. By restructuring a couple of job roles and promoting onsite shift supervisors to work under Tara, Tara's employer was able to retain Tara remotely. The transition was implemented without any disruption to the clinics under her supervision. As of today, Tara does all the practice administration, business development, and other supervisory tasks from a distance, and the day-to-day onsite work is handled by her shift supervisors who have flourished. Tara comes into town once a quarter for face time with everyone and everything is going great!

Businesses now have a unique opportunity to rethink traditional staffing and retention models by leveraging this moment in history in creative ways. Because businesses pivoted to survive 2020, much of the change management work needed to overcome that resistance to remote work has already occurred. Remote leaders that learn to evaluate their people based on performance rather than work location can develop vital, learning organizations with their existing teams. Remote leaders who focus on all their people can access team talent more easily, utilize everyone's strengths, and gain more ROI (Return on Investment) from their full workforce without adding overhead cost. This approach provides greater workforce equity and encourages inclusion as it focuses on objective measures like job performance, talent, and capabilities. For most companies, payroll is a company's biggest line-item expense. Improved employee productivity adds business value without adding any additional expense to your balance sheet. Plus, there is a direct correlation between remote team engagement and improved team productivity making this an appealing business strategy.

There are additional benefits to using this operating model. Companies that implement them see unexpected productivity gains in their in-person office employees as well as their remote employees. This is because well designed, well executed remote work systems hold everyone to the same standard across your workforce. It elevates performance expectations for everyone as there is more emphasis on work delivery and greater recognition of utilization of everyone's strengths and talents. This only happens when company leaders transform their management style, so it aligns and supports the team as a whole.

A Remote Workforce Is a More Adaptive Workforce

Remote professionals are inherently self-sufficient problem-solvers, adapting to whatever is thrown at them. Most are curious and active learners, used to change and pivots. This makes remote employees less change resistant if they understand the context for the change and it makes logical sense to them. Conversely, they are more change resistant if there is poor communication as to the reason for the change, or the change seems illogical or ill-conceived to them. Companies with remote employees that use the remote employee's problem-solving capabilities to help organize and implement needed operational changes design better solutions that are less disruptive to the business, gain better adoption, and pivot quicker. Remote employees familiar with the work functions can help design better change solutions that are functionally sound, helping companies to avoid costly operational disruptions. These same employees are better change implementers as they can work through functional problems quickly and provide reliable information to their remote colleagues. They are also better trainers as they can speak more credibly to the realities of working remotely.

I used this approach with one client, a national hearing aid distributor with over a 100 retail clinics located along the US east coast. Each retail clinic had minimal staff, usually two, no more than three employees, a hearing clinician, occasionally a technician, and a customer service representative (CSR) that managed the office administrative tasks such as scheduling, billing, and patient follow-ups. Traditionally, all new hire training took place in-person, face-to-face. The training process required an existing CSR to travel to the newly hired CSR's location and stay with the new CSR onsite for a brief period. Once training was completed, the new CSR was left on their own with minimal support. Any follow-up happened via email or phone calls (if it happened at all). Over the years, due to changes in insurance paperwork, documentation requirements, and other business factors, the CSR role had grown into a complex, nuanced job that required a CSR to self-organize and work independently even as they learned the ins and outs of the business. Unsurprisingly, they had lots of questions, and many new CSRs got overwhelmed quickly resulting in poor work performance, improper paperwork, and high turnover. The CSR trainers, typically high performers responsible for their own clinics as well as providing support for the CSRs, were suffering burn out because of the travel and increased workload. Because of high CSR turnover, trainers traveled a lot and their clinics suffered because of their absence. The company paid the price in increasing hiring and training costs as well as continually disrupted clinical operations.

I worked with the client to stop this vicious cycle by strategically rethinking ways to restructure CSR training utilizing their trainers differently. We started by building the technical infrastructure e.g., webcams, video conferencing software, reliable internet capabilities, laptops, etc. at the clinic level that enabled face-to-face communication and screen sharing for distance support and remote learning sessions. Then we recruited a small, dedicated group of top CSRs that were located regionally and provided them with specialized training in remote team business skills e.g., remote teaching, distance communications, providing support online, managing relationships, and delivering feedback at a distance. We used this group to help us redesign the CSR new hire training process and to create a remote clinical support process to cover clinics when trainers were absent or to staff a clinic when a CSR left the company. These CSR trainers still spent some time onsite with a new CSR employee, but they were able to reduce the in-person time without losing contact as some training got converted to eLearning self-study and some to livestream video training with screen sharing. This new system allowed new CSRs to learn how to function independently quicker by providing them with real-time mentoring via video and screen sharing when questions arose. The new CSRs felt supported because they could reach out to their trainer via technology and get answers quickly and they were more engaged in company initiatives because the CSR trainers were communicating new initiatives to their colleagues in their regions. CSR trainers spent less time away from their clinics reducing the amount of operational disruption.

The program resulted in a reduction in CSR turnover and greater stability operationally across the company. New CSRs felt more supported and less overwhelmed plus they felt part of a team. The cost savings that resulted allowed the company to increase CSR trainer wages to align with their new value. The CSR trainers were so respected by the company leaders that it wasn't long before the training team got pulled into a bunch of new initiatives. Between new hire training, the CSR trainers were often called upon to provide mentoring to existing CSRs who had skill gaps or suffered from performance issues. Earning a spot on the training team became a desired position that helped CSRs see a path forward for career advancement and this energized the most talented CSRs across the company to step up their game.

The CSR training team became such an operational asset that when the company had to rollout a complicated new operating system, the CSR training team helped design new workflows, built all the training materials for the new system, provided all the functional technical training for all company CSRs via livestream video, then they staffed the field support effort and held daily livestream video Q&A sessions to answer questions and troubleshoot. The result was a major technology upgrade that rolled out with minimal business disruption and was an unmitigated business success.

To Achieve These Results, Prepare to Re-Tool Your Mindset and Your Operations

You can't achieve any of these gains without changing your operating model and your mindset. Companies that successfully adopt remote work operating models acknowledge the unique needs of remote teams and adjust their operating practices to proactively address the unique attributes of remote work. Use this handbook to create your own roadmap for making the shift. You will notice I talk a lot about change management in this book. For existing businesses, making strategic choices of this type will mean managing change with your people. I want to make sure you plan for it in advance, so you are ready when the inevitable challenges come. You will find that your existing remote employees are more willing than most employees to try new things if they perceive the change will improve their work process, give them more work efficiencies, or solve a perceived pain point. To convert this energy into positive business results, prepare to create operational mechanisms for your remote employees to contribute their ideas in productive, meaningful ways.

Why Adopt Remote Work as a Business Strategy Now?

Because you are more than halfway there already. The year 2020 forced many businesses to give remote work a try. Remote work is more common than ever before and if you have multiple locations, a dispersed team, work from home policies, or your people work on the road while they travel, you are well on your way. However, adopting remote work strategies and optimizing them for improved business results takes commitment, an open-mind, and a willingness to invest time and resources. You will need to build the infrastructure, adjust old or design new work processes, learn new leadership models, then implement personal accountability measures for yourself and your people to get yourself all the way to strategic remote work. This may seem like a lot of effort, but the payoffs are worth it. No one is suggesting you can do this overnight. Remember the old saying: "How do you eat an elephant?" Answer: "One bite at a time." That's what this handbook does, it breaks down the process systematically so you can follow along and build your plan to formalize remote work with a clear end goal in mind.

Timelines for implementing your plan will depend on your circumstances, your team's openness to change, and your ability to lead that change. The year 2020 created an overnight mental shift for many that did some of the hard work for you. If your teams worked remotely during 2020, then you have proof of concept, and a significant percentage of your people are probably already onboard. In fact, trying to bring them back into an office is insulting as many team members proved they can meet, and even exceed, performance expectations working remotely. Eliminating a remote work option sends the message you don't trust them when they are out of your sight. Remember, traditionally, folks working outside the "home office" often felt less valued because traditional organizational cultures viewed them with suspicion and assumed them guilty without just cause. Enforcing mandatory return-to-the-office policies confirms a lack of trust for remote employees. Not a positive message to send.

Today these same remote employees have recognized their market value and feel empowered to push back. Employees are demanding more flexibility from their employers and, if employers continue to dismiss, disrespect, or demean them, they will take their talents and go elsewhere. As more organizations choose to implement flexible work arrangements, they will become immediately attractive to the brightest talent seeking remote work options. Currently, the technical ecosystem for enabling remote work is cost-effective and widely available. Moreover, 2020 proved many more jobs than previously assumed can be performed remotely. So, there really isn't a plausible rationale for going back to an all in-person office workplace in the future.

A growing number of companies are paying attention to this shift. There is a growing market for remote work-related products, job boards focused on remote work options, and specialized business skills training focused on remote work. That means improved tools, new product offerings, and access to remote work alternatives are coming fast. This market demand will make it easier and more cost-effective for anyone to get onboard – employers and employees alike. You have a small window to take the leap, be a pioneer, and become one of these preferred employers. Do the work now, proactively plan your future on your terms, and implement on your timeline or get forced into it tomorrow after your competitors beat you to it and leave you forever playing catch-up. It's up to you.

Highlights

Remote work takes many forms. For this handbook, I define remote work as any work team that shares three characteristics.

- ■ Some or all the team members are physically separated in some way and do not share the same physical workspace at the same time.
- ■ Team interactions, communication, collaboration, and work processes are enabled by and dependent upon technology, both hardware and software, and the internet.

■ Team members are real, live people that must ignore distance and utilize technology to form effective working relationships and execute their work obligations.

There are many compelling reasons for adopting a remote work business strategy.

■ It helps you access the talent of your existing remote workers.
■ Highly skilled remote employees add high value and need less managing.
■ Retaining valuable remote talent is a smart cost-savings strategy.
■ A remote workforce is a more adaptive workforce.

Why adopt a remote work strategy now?

■ Because you are already halfway there, and you don't even know it.
■ Your current organization isn't structured to reap the full benefits of remote work, but there is still time to be a leader in this space.
■ This handbook outlines the steps needed to implement, operationalize, and optimize a remote work operating model.

Note

1. The systems introduced in this handbook will work for all forms of remote work that fit this standardized definition with minor adjustments for your unique circumstances.

Chapter 2

Build It Right

Identify the Remote Work Operating Model that Is Right for You

Lots of people ask me if it's necessary to make the organizational changes I outline in this handbook, to accommodate remote teams. Yes, it is. No matter how long you may have had remote employees in your company, it's unlikely your current structure fully accommodates, recognizes, or supports anyone working outside of your home office. This is not unusual as organizations rarely leverage their remote employees strategically. They are an undervalued, untapped resource. Very few companies consciously design a supportive remote work business model focused on leveraging the potential of every remote employee to their fullest value. Companies are currently losing opportunities to apply their remote workers' unique skills and talents to the company's existing challenges. It's more likely the current company leadership dismisses remote workers as less diligent or treats them with outright suspicion. Since there is rarely a formal remote work structure, even though some form of remote work is now part of almost every workplace, it's probable you are missing potential security and liability risks lurking within your infrastructure. Since remote employees are largely ignored and are rarely part of most companies' strategic plan, remote work employees are left to create their own systems and workarounds to get things done. Not addressing the fundamentals leaves you vulnerable. You need to assess and address all this structurally before you can reap the benefits and achieve sustainable business gains from remote work.

DOI: 10.4324/9781003243557-2

Building out the structure to suit your needs is a necessary and key step as it will mentally prepare you and your team for the operational changes and the new leadership and teamwork approaches. There is always room to tailor things to suit your situation. And it's natural you will make compromises based on your circumstances and operational constraints. I've made sure to emphasize where you can cut corners safely and where you must not. As a pragmatic businessperson who lives most of my life in the real world of ambiguous gray, I do believe everything in business is a judgment call. I'm also a firm believer in avoiding change just for change's sake. I often urge clients to repurpose existing systems, hold on to old technology that is still business-sound, and leave existing workflows alone if they function well or they are bound by unbreakable contract agreements. But I do challenge you to look carefully at everything with a fresh set of eyes. Don't keep hold of something because it's safe and comfortable, make the hard business decisions with an eye to the future you want to build, and you will get much better results in the long run.

Start with the End in Mind, then Recruit Help

I talk a lot about change in this book because operationalizing a new remote work business model is a major change effort. Building a remote work-centric company represents a shift in thinking and operational practice and many people will resist this change if you let them. I told you at the beginning, that managing people is the hardest part of your job. I wasn't kidding. So, the remainder of this chapter is devoted to preliminary activities that lay the groundwork for successful implementation and operationalization while addressing the change management considerations. You must plan for them up front to drive adoption for your new remote work model. Don't skip this part as it is a necessary step in the process, and it will make operationalizing your plan easier down the road.

Start with the end goal in mind and really think through your business reasons for adopting this change. Devise your long-term vision for your remote work business model in a way that supports both your business goals and the type of business culture you wish to cultivate (Figure 2.1). Both are an important starting point. Don't feel pressure to decide every little detail as your goals will shift and adjust along the way as you learn things and get input from others. Keep in mind perfection is the enemy of good enough. All you need is enough details to allow you to effectively communicate a convincing high-level vision and gain initial buy-in. To start this process, I always ask myself a simple question – where do I want my organization, company, and team to be in 12–24 months from today? And in the next 2–3 years from now, and beyond? I add my business aspirations, service goals, team interaction goals, learning goals, etc. that are

Remote Team Operating Model
Build Your Virtual Office

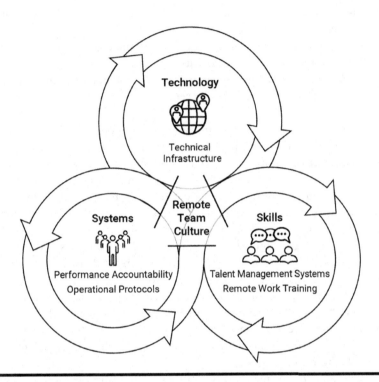

Figure 2.1 A strategically planned remote work operating model will support both your business goals and the type of business culture you wish to cultivate.

commensurate with my yearly business goals. For example, my long-term vision for my own remote work company includes:

- cost-effective, flexible, high quality service delivery that is client focused;
- a lean core team that uses select subcontractors to scale quickly when we take on bigger projects;
- low fixed costs and minimal operational overhead;
- a talent recruiting strategy based on individual capabilities and remote work competencies;
- a company culture based on a mutual respect for difference;
- a focus on continual individual and team learning;

- an open-minded approach to problem-solving;
- a transparent, mature approach to interpersonal communication;
- a secure business infrastructure that protects our company and our client's data;
- team resilience that embraces change and sees the value in continually evolving ourselves and our products and services;
- a continued model that allows us to address these goals as a remote team with maximum workplace flexibility;
- plus, business growth goals that are realistic but a bit of a stretch to keep things challenged but realistically centered.

Make your own list based on your business aspirations. If you have an existing well-defined vision and detailed strategic plan, it may make sense for you to use them as a starting point, then re-adjust, re-design, or simply tweak to accommodate remote work. For some of you, you may find it necessary to start from scratch as your current business strategy can't or won't accommodate or support remote work. Your list is important as it is the basis for recruiting support and buy-in for the change. The goals help you prioritize and allocate resources in a mindful way. They provide a baseline to measure progress and help you define meaningful success metrics as you transform your vision into business strategy and tactical implementation plans. You will need all these elements to keep people motivated and enthusiastic because operationalizing a vision is really demanding work. It requires focus and a clear road map with a clear end destination. Proactively designing your long-term vision helps you anticipate and address concerns ahead of time and that is a lot less disruptive on your people and your business.

You are going to hear me say this a lot - proactive planning is less disruptive, more cost-effective, and easier on everyone, including you. Period. I've worked with a lot of people in my time, who enjoy creating chaos as a distraction to avoid change. These folks lack the foresight or planning talent to organize in advance, or worse, they are adrenaline junkies who swoop in at the moment of crisis to save the day then blame others for the fallout that they, themselves, created. They do it to gratify their own egos because they never develop the requisite leadership skills to run an efficient operation, or they are bad at holding themselves and their employees accountable. These tactics are a needless and exhausting waste of business resources that exact a terrible toll on the hardworking people stuck running day-to-day operations or working to implement change. It is a needless, costly, and psychologically demoralizing way to run a business. You'll have a lot less drama if you take the time to plan up front. The best kind of rollout is the one that takes place with minimal crisis and leaves the rollout team proud of themselves and confident enough to take on new challenges. Everything I've laid out for you in this handbook is geared toward this goal – a healthy, human-friendly, profitable work environment that energizes the people in it.

Take a Multi-Discipline Approach, But Assign a Remote Work Champion to Lead

Building, implementing, and operationalizing an effective remote work business model is no joke. Plan on recruiting a multi-disciplinary coalition, as you will need all the help you can get to make it happen. The five components I mentioned earlier in this chapter will touch every aspect of your business and require experts from every imaginable discipline. During my corporate days, I often relied on steering committees and/or multi-disciplinary working groups to assist me with major change projects like this. I used them to expedite operational decision-making, to create project momentum, and to encourage broad buy-in within the rank and file. I have some smart clients who have taken this to the next level and created remote work "super user" groups within key areas like the IT Help Desk, Operations, Finance, Legal, Risk, Compliance, and HR for extended field support. I advise all my clients undertaking remote work implementations to think about all these options. Regardless of what you call them, these distinct types of coalitions and working groups provide vital business advantages:

1. Participation makes individual participants a part of the process, giving them a personal stake in the project's success as it ties their work goals to the implementation.
2. You get the benefit of each participant's expertise from the beginning.
3. Participants get exposure to working collaboratively with folks from outside their disciplines and it leads to a great respect for difference.
4. Participants get exposure to a lot of new things, build skills, and learn a lot in the process.
5. You don't have to shoulder the workload alone and change can move forward faster because you have help.
6. Having a multi-disciplinary team gives the project more legitimacy and greater integrity.
7. You have other voices who can speak on behalf of the project and address skeptics and naysayers when you aren't available to do so.

While coalitions of all types are vital, you will need someone to lead the charge, provide vision and goals, guide the team, and remind team members over and over of that future vision. Choose a remote work champion with strong leadership skills, change management experience, emotional intelligence, project management capabilities, critical thinking, and multi-channel communication skills. This is a significant skill set because leading change of this type has big implications for the company long term. If you are unable to find one person with the requisite skills, form a working group around these skills. Once you have your champion(s), grant them the authority, resources, and budget they will need to get the job done right. Your designated champion(s) must build coalition cohesion, rally everyone to the project mission, and engage additional working groups who will be hesitant and anxious at first. Your change champion(s) will be one of the most important decisions you will make. Don't cut corners. Once you have a champion, introduce them to your coalitions as they will work together collaboratively to define the specific implementation pathway and identify the functional priorities associated with each of the five components. It's your remote work champion's role to leverage these coalition and work groups wisely and gain their buy-in for the final plan as things move forward.

It's hard for many people to advance in unison if they don't see the central vision and have one central voice constantly re-stating the end goal and directing people's efforts toward it. The US military is one of the world's largest remote work organizations in existence. They define a mission, assign roles, designate a clear chain of command, and drive execution through their processes and procedures. It's the ultimate multi-disciplinary remote team organization. When you pull together these first remote work project teams, your day-to-day team interactions will be a little messy because your people aren't military recruits. Your remote work champion(s) will oversee directing the action. Your champion(s) must have the authority to make operational decisions and ready access to top level decision-makers to resolve issues quickly as they arise. There is a time for listening to build consensus and there is a time for decisive action to maintain momentum and keep things moving forward. You need a remote work champion(s) who is adept at balancing the two to run this project effectively.

Recruit from the Top, Middle, and Line Level

Clients ask me when they can start recruiting their change champion(s) and their coalition. My answer is simple, as quickly as possible, and as early in the process as you can. As this is a substantial change management project, look for people who are energized by or see the future opportunity in the change or people already engaged in remote work. Leverage your internal and external networks for the right talent. Look for people with expertise from all five components. Recruit subject matter experts (SMEs) who are traditional office workers but who have an open mind about remote work. Seek out reasonable skeptics who may need convincing but who are willing to give you the benefit of the doubt up front or people who trust you and will try it on your say so. Whenever possible, include employees who are remote workers with established reputations, have functional expertise, and are well regarded by their peers. Choose new, young talent with experience working collaboratively online through school projects or other activities. Then identify key remote work experts, consultants, and contractors to fill in the gaps. Remote work experts like me work with our clients to help them accelerate planning and avoid basic pitfalls. Plus, we have a network of strategic partners who pay attention to recent advances or policy changes related to remote work. We have exposure to the many ways people are integrating remote work and we can offer creative ways to solve your pain points quickly and efficiently.

Ultimately, your goal is to create a highly diverse group of hand-picked early adopters and "convertibles" willing to participate in your plan. Think about skills, mind sets, and choose change champions and coalition candidates from all levels of the organization. Later, in Chapter 8, when we discuss the use of pilot programs to test ideas, you will understand why you need this diverse group. These folks you recruit early on are an incredibly valuable resource whose business value grows over time. These first recruits will become your remote work "super users" supporting the larger company rollout as it gains momentum. They will role model the new culture; become the reliable spokespeople for change; provide real life examples of how the system works; and deliver real time, relevant operations feedback throughout implementation so problems can be addressed quickly. I utilize them for group training, peer mentoring, ongoing support, project communications, reporting, and other important rollout activities. Many of the people I have recruited for these types of projects find they enjoy the change process. I've seen many of them go on to become significant, influential change leaders, helping their organization navigate future changes with great skill.

Seek Support and Buy-in from Executive Sponsors and Key Stakeholders

In addition to your initial change champion(s) and coalition recruits; executive sponsors and key stakeholders play a vital role in implementing a remote work business model. These are the people in charge of corporate strategy and decision-making with big budgets and lots of clout. Look for senior executives who have a lot of motivation to provide support to ensure implementation success. Business owners, C-suite executives, Presidents, Executive Directors, etc. whose performance is judged on the bottom-line results. Your coalition members may be more useful when it comes to helping you operationalize a remote work business model, but it will be hard to gain the unilateral decision authority, meaningful coalition participation, and needed budget support without these folks at the top.

Key stakeholders are senior leaders, but they serve a slightly different purpose. They may own responsibilities for critical systems, workflow, or access to resources or data e.g., IT, HR, Finance, Operations, etc. They may be indirectly impacted by remote work, but their resistance to it will create big problems for the project. It's highly unlikely you can convince an entire senior leadership team as often there are multiple conflicting agendas at play. I've only seen it happen once in my career. It's more likely you will need to construct a compelling business case and work to convince a couple of key players to step up. If that's the case, choose one or two critical decision-makers with budget responsibility who are functionally knowledgeable that other leaders trust (or at minimum respect). Look for a senior leader who will consider the business benefits, see the business advantages, and will keep an open mind. Choose an executive sponsor that other leaders will listen to and take seriously if they endorse your new remote work model. If you can find key stakeholders with business challenges that remote work can address e.g., critical staffing deficits that are hard to fill with local talent or someone whose business group is in distress so they may see your plan as a viable way forward. This may be an operations manager whose budget cuts who might see remote work as a compelling business case.

I hope the biggest message you've taken from this chapter is once you decide to adopt a remote work business model there is a lot of work to do before you design, implement, or operationalize your new remote work business plan. But proactive planning, besides being less disruptive and less costly, improves your chances for faster adoption and gives you 10× return on investment down the road. This is a skill worth developing as this entire implementation process is reusable for future business rollouts. It doesn't just apply to remote work implementations. As team development is a core part of this approach, there are ancillary business benefits that last well beyond this implementation. The advanced skills you and your team learn will contribute to productivity gains, improved team resilience, and greater team capabilities over time.

Highlights

Identify the remote work operating model that is right for you

- Businesses rarely leverage the full value of their remote employees and, as a result, they fail to capture potential revenue and strategic advantages from their remote workforce.

- It's necessary to take the time to assess and address the structural needs of remote work to maximum business opportunities while mitigating potential business risks.
- Every business will have unique business requirements that affect the remote work operating model. Prepare to build the one that best suits your business needs.

Start with the end in mind, then recruit help

- Establish your long-term vision for the shift then identify the business and cultural objectives you wish to achieve.
- Build your remote work strategy so it supports and aligns with your vision, business, and cultural objectives.
- Start with questions – where do I want my team to be in the short term (12–24 months) and the long term (next 2–3 years)?
- Proactive planning is less disruptive, more cost-effective, and easier on everyone, including you.

Take a multi-discipline approach, but assign a remote work champion to lead

- Building your remote work operating model will impact all aspects of your business and require a multi-disciplined approach.
- Appoint a remote work champion and grant them the authority to lead the change.
- Recruit carefully as this team will play a big part in the success of your plan.

Recruit from the top, middle, and line level

- This implementation will benefit from an implementation team comprised of a variety of backgrounds and functional expertise.
- Use this opportunity to appoint people that will benefit from the experience and who will continue to add value beyond the implementation.

Seek support and buy-in from executive sponsors and key stakeholders

- Seek the support of key executives and stakeholders that can provide needed resources, experience, and a political foundation for the change.
- Recruit early adopters and open-minded skeptics that are well regarded and respected within the organization to help champion the change.

Chapter 3

The Five Organizational Components of Remote Work

When you take the leap and adopt a remote work operating model, it's important you familiarize yourself with the organizational components necessary to support daily work. Because a remote team works in multiple locations, these components create a virtual office that your remote employees share. This is important. Without something to bind them, each employee will work independently without understanding how they fit in, how their work contributes, and how their actions impact others. Misunderstandings fueled by a lack of trust among the team occur frequently because individual team members lack empathy for each other. It's hard to feel empathy for strangers, we're not naturally hardwired for it, there must be some catalyst for it to occur and it takes active leadership to sustain it. Without a virtual office structure to connect them, remote employees work in a lonely vacuum. Since there is no meaningful connection, engagement and commitment are low. It's easy for remote employees to leave because there is no emotional connection. The emotional cost of departure is minimal. To help you in your virtual office planning, I've laid out the five components (Figure 3.1) that address the structural needs necessary to create team connection and enable sustainable, productive remote work. Those components are:

1. **infrastructure;**
2. **operational protocols;**
3. **performance accountability measures;**

DOI: 10.4324/9781003243557-3

4. **talent management systems;**
5. **workforce skill building.**

Each component is essential for remote work success. Make sure to account for them in your operationalization plans, as well as your implementation and ongoing maintenance budgets to ensure you have a stable foundation that aligns with and supports the needs of your remote workforce. I've done deep dives detailing each component in Chapters 4 through 8. As you read through these chapters, you will notice there are lots of crossover areas between components.

The Five Organizational Components of Remote Work

Outfitting Your Virtual Office for Remote Team Success

Your Remote Team

5 Skill Building

4 Talent Management Systems

3 Accountability

2 Operational Protocols

1 Technical Infrastructure

Figure 3.1   These five components address the structural needs of your remote team.

That's how it is. No component exists entirely on its own. Rather, together they are integrated. You are striving for interoperability. A seamless structure that functions like a remote team, working in unison with each component playing its part. Once you define your business goals and strategic plan, you may need to reorganize or customize these components to suit your unique circumstances. I've included a high-level summary checklist pointing out critical priorities at the end of each chapter to make it easy for you.

Highlights

There are five operational components of remote work discussed in this handbook. Over the next five chapters I discuss them in detail. They include:

- infrastructure;
- operational protocols;
- performance accountability measures;
- talent management systems;
- workforce skill building.

Chapter 4

Component One: Infrastructure

Remote work is possible today because of the global accessibility of the internet and technology advances in both hardware and software. Remote work stops when the internet or the technical infrastructure fails, so it's important to a) build it right, b) create a plan to maintain it, and c) continue to perpetually invest in it as it is a business necessity for your remote teams. As technology changes, so will your remote work infrastructure. This is not a static environment; it is dynamic and ever changing. Every organization must make strategic choices as to how they accommodate this and, for better or for worse, there are a lot of options today. Better, because of the array of cost-effective options. Worse, because it can feel overwhelming if you are a non-technical person to navigate a cloud-based landscape.

A quick disclaimer, there is no one way to accomplish remote work infrastructure and I don't intend to do a deep dive into today's specific infrastructure technology choices as the choices are endless and changing by the minute. Nor do I have specific technical or product recommendations. If I do reference a product, it's to highlight a concept. It's not an endorsement. I'm not a network administrator, cloud computing, cybersecurity, or a technology expert and don't claim to be. My goal is to elevate your awareness of the important part technology plays in remote work. Technical infrastructure is a necessary component and I'm starting with it because remote work can't exist without it. I want to provide you with enough background so you can ask the right questions of the experts you consult as part of your planning process. Most businesses will leverage third-party solutions for some or all their remote work infrastructure. Finding reputable options is vital. To do this, you need to know some of the basics.

DOI: 10.4324/9781003243557-4

Every remote work organization these days leverages internet service providers (ISPs) and the cloud in some way. But there is no single configuration. Your infrastructure must complement your business objectives. You will need help building it, testing it, deploying it, keeping it secure, and maintaining it. There are lots of ways to do this. Some companies invest in a capable internal team. This team will look quite different than previous network administration teams that supported a traditional hardwired on-premises local area network (LAN). Today's IT (Information Technology) teams are much smaller and more reliant on technical versatility, and critical thinking skills. They must be good problem solvers and keep learning new, emerging technology trends to stay ahead of new technology to maintain their relevance. Some companies outsource everything through strategic partnerships with third party IT Service Management (ITSM) technology vendors. Most companies have a cobbled together solution that combines the two.

Everything I discuss in this chapter has distinct pros and cons for your business. It's not for me to say which one is best for you. I'm highlighting the components to ensure you include them in your plan and ensure you have what you need to do your due diligence during your implementation. I've defined infrastructure as one big technology component that encompasses internet connectivity, hardware, software, strategy, support, system/business processes, and security. This is because interoperability – the seamless knitting of many systems so they work effectively as one integrated system supports your remote work business operation. In preparation for this chapter, I reached out to several trusted chief information officer (CIO) colleagues and expert technology partners to get their perspective on remote work infrastructure today, and I've synthesized their feedback into the following categories:

- networks, the cloud, and business system access,
- devices, apps, and backups,
- systems, data, and IP security,
- legal, compliance, and regulatory considerations – a shifting landscape,
- role of the help desk,
- business continuity planning post-2020.

Networks, the Cloud, and Business System Access

The advances in network technologies, internet accessibility and capabilities, and the growth of the cloud computing industry have made remote work easier than ever. For someone like me who has managed remote teams for over 20 years, this is an exciting and encouraging evolutionary shift. Honestly, it is hard to imagine how we managed remote work before the current technology existed. So much more is possible now and there are so many interesting, cool options. Organizations located just about anywhere in the world now have cost effective choices available to them. No matter your size, large or small, determining the right remote work infrastructure solution for your organization is easier when you have clearly defined end goals. Once you have goals, you can evaluate your infrastructure options and make your decisions based on critical business factors like budget, security requirements, geographic considerations, technical requirements, business requirements, and overall operating objectives. Solutions will change as you scale or your business shifts or you add new products and services. You could choose a simple cloud-based virtual workspace for a small team, a third-party ITSM product as you grow, or an internal virtual appliance infrastructure (VMware) for scale. But it's more likely you will have some combination thereof with lots more software-as-a-service (SaaS) add-ons and apps that address different aspects of your specific business needs. Remote work does require, at minimum, specific infrastructure that supports consistent and dependable remote work system access, defined workflows, and team communications. As I mentioned earlier, every infrastructure choice comes with pro and con trade-offs and when designed poorly, infrastructure can work against you and have costly consequences. Take the time to educate yourself and/or seek the guidance of knowledgeable, up-to-date practitioners you trust.

Infrastructure includes internet accessibility and user network connectivity as the internet is the point of entry for your remote work system users. You need to learn about mobile device management (MDM), virtual desktops, cloud storage, remote access protocols (RAP) as they may become part of your plan. Since teams are dependent on video technology to meet and stay engaged, you will need video conferencing software, web cameras, headsets, and microphones. Whatever tools you choose need to be accessible to every member of the team in their geography. If your team is international, think global. While the internet is theoretically available everywhere, it doesn't mean every employee's access is equal. Don't assume. Test, test, test. Learn the technical, regulatory, and governmental considerations impacting your employees. These things aren't unique to remote teams. You will have the same needs if your office team uses laptops, tablets, or cell phones outside the office e.g., for business travel or hold meetings via video to stay in touch with each other or with customers. Today's workforce is mobile and technology dependent. Anything you build for your remote teams now will also benefit your in-person office staff and will provide a host of versatile options for connecting with customers, vendors, and contractors. Be prepared for more change soon. Tomorrow's technology is already on the path to commercialization. The metaverse will add additional demands on your infrastructure as business starts experimenting with more immersive technology.

I predict virtual reality, augmented reality, and artificial intelligence will play a big part in the workplace of the future.

For non-technologists all this can be very intimidating. Having knowledgeable technology advisors is critical. Where do you find reliable technology subject matter experts you can trust? I'm constantly on the lookout for them and seek them out as part of my business strategy. I make a point of cultivating relationships with respected, trust-worthy technologists that I meet while speaking at professional organizations or through my client work (I called several of them to ask their advice for this book). Vendors have valuable information, too, but their goal is to sell solutions, so while I learn about products from vendors, I try to stay technology agnostic because technology products change so fast and there really is no single product or service that addresses everything. I work hard to stay on top of technology trends by subscribing to news sources that report on technology innovations and technology failures. I listen to podcasts, read blogs, attend webinars, and seek out other networking organizations that keep these topics top of mind. This background work helps me evaluate what I'm hearing from my network. When I am looking for the best fit for my company or advising a client, I've got lots of trusted sources to consult because I cultivated them ahead of time. Finally, I always seek out the users of any technical solutions under consideration to ask for their feedback so I can evaluate the real-life application experience and separate that from the sales hype before making final recommendations.

Because today's remote work infrastructure consists of multi-product solutions, it's important to test the end-to-end process to ensure everything functions as planned. My friend, Dave H, stresses the importance of system interoperability. Dave is the CIO of a healthcare organization. In his world, interoperability refers to timely and secure access, integration, and the secure access of electronic health data across his entire system so that it can be used to optimize health outcomes for individuals and populations. For other service organizations it refers to the seamless system integration that supports end-to-end optimal workflow and employee productivity that is secure and reduces business risk. For customer service and retail organizations, interoperability might include the customer experience as well as the employee experience. Dave always says to me, "IT is here to serve the end user of our systems and those impacted by our services, not the other way around." So, it's important to consult your end users early and include them in the design and implementation process If you want a solution that truly supports workflow and operational needs and is functionally sound. Your multi-disciplinary coalitions that I alluded to in Chapter 2 can test the end-to-end process and give you feedback on the user experience so you can establish an acceptable balance between productivity and security as you build out your remote work infrastructure.

Devices, Apps, and Backups

Laptops, tablets, and cell phones allow remote work to take place anywhere there is internet access or cellular service. Mobile devices, particularly smartphones, changed the game for remote work. They are lighter, more powerful, and better designed for use on the go. Cell phones have opened remote work business opportunities in unique ways, and they are redefining what it means to work remotely. In many cultures, they are now more prevalent than laptops and tablets as the device of choice. There is a whole community of remote professionals known as "digital nomads" that are creating remote work ecosystems across the globe. I know one amazing woman named Miss Lin who lives in a rural mountain village in northwest Vietnam near Sapa. Miss Lin's village has no electricity, running water, and no Wi-Fi connection, yet she runs a very successful tourist guide service completely through her cell phone. I also know a very tech-savvy C-suite executive from a well-known tech company who likes traveling to exotic, distant places yet keeps up with his business responsibilities using only his cell phone. He once wired one million dollars to an organization located in Boston, MA as he was mountain climbing in Asia.

As you build your remote work plan for your company, devices are an essential part of the puzzle. Devices are physical objects that can be stolen, damaged, corrupted, hacked, or simply wear out. You need processes for purchasing them, configuring them, getting them into the hands of your remote employees, servicing them, replacing them when they fail, and, if lost or stolen, locating them, or wiping their data remotely. Devices may be small, but they are highly sophisticated computers containing a lot of data. They are points of entry to your critical business systems, making them a point of vulnerability for system security. They contain business sensitive information that must be backed up and operating systems and apps that need updating regularly. This includes cell phones. Many businesses forget to do backups on mobile devices, yet we keep lots of business sensitive data on our devices, business contacts, electronic calendars, passwords, it goes on and on. Make sure you don't get caught – add cell phone backups to your technical system backup and security plans.

Devices are also complicated as there is no universal standard for electronics and everyone has their own preferences as to what they like. Chargers, batteries, and accessories are unique to a device and will need replacing if the device is replaced. Mobile networks are different from Wi-Fi and when your employees have multiple devices, as they invariably do these days, all these devices need to sync. Electricity and internet bandwidth aren't universal either. Different countries have different electrical systems and different internet infrastructure. If your team is global and you are purchasing in bulk, appreciate the implications and plan for them. We have apps for everything these days, and they are popular business work tools. The apps you adopt need to be added to every work device, synced between work devices, and updated continually to keep them secure. Take all of this into consideration as you make your plan.

Systems, Data, and IP Security

Technology systems have vulnerabilities of all kinds. There is no getting around this. It's pretty much an accepted fact that we have surpassed a threshold where it's no longer "if" an organization will have a breach or a technical system failure of some kind, but "when." Regardless of the systems or third-party vendors you use, the products you choose, the steps you take, CIOs and other cybersecurity professionals across all industries advise organizations to adopt a zero-trust security strategy and plan for failure in advance of an attack. Ironically, vulnerabilities exist whether you are in an office or working in a remote team so you can't ignore this. Where you have people, you have exposure. Don't delude yourself into thinking that you are safe. Something is always happening in your organization that puts you at risk, you just don't know it. Adopting a remote work strategy that plans for trouble gives you an opportunity to conduct a full assessment of top system vulnerabilities so you can educate yourself and your employees. Develop a good plan for mitigating those risks as much as you can by preparing for problems before they happen.

Top security vulnerabilities include:

1. Old, unpatched, or outdated systems that harbor unsuspected vulnerabilities.
2. Human error through a) weak or insecure passwords, b) the sending of sensitive information to the wrong recipients, and/or c) phishing scams.
3. Malware introduced via devices with unapproved downloads, poor system management, or third-party vendors.
4. Insider misuse e.g., when an approved system user either deliberately or unwittingly creates a system problem.
5. Physical theft of a carry device e.g., cell phone, tablet, or laptop.

For anyone who went remote in 2020, there is a particular need for concern. Many organizations who sent employees home at that time, did so without an advanced plan. The shift to remote was an emergency response necessary for business survival. Often technical solutions were cobbled together quickly without due diligence or end-to-end testing. Many employees had to get creative and adopted emergency workarounds to get work done and keep the business going. Most of them used their personal devices, home Wi-Fi, and their technology was accessible to other members of their household. Every one of these choices has inherent risk. If you haven't done so already, assess your current situation against the process outlined in this book. It will help you to identify problems that you can address in the short term while you construct your long-term remote work strategy.

I will continue to stress the need for a multi-functional coalition approach for these assessments because of the never-ending tension between security concerns and efficient workflow. Invest in these relationships early on and get your experts working together because this tension will continually increase given the cybersecurity concerns that are on the rise. More cyber-crime means more security systems and protocols. Yet VPNs, dual authentication, password verification, and advanced system security all slow down work systems and will affect business productivity and workflow creating high stress and frustration for your remote employees. Modernize your environment for resiliency and system security through a secure cloud environment, smart apps, and robust end user support but never forget IT exists to enable business-critical activities that generate the revenue to keep your business running.

While many CIOs are pressed to adopt a "zero-trust security strategy" that assumes the worst, there must be a balance. If the system is so locked down that work can't advance, that's a problem. Having everyone in the room in advance, investing up front in security monitoring so the company can catch problems as fast as possible while also enabling team productivity will take creative, collaborative compromise solutions that recognize the business realities from all sides of the problem. None of this can happen if you don't plan in advance. Don't skimp on this, it's too important.

Make sure any infrastructure security plan includes the following:

1. **Provide an ongoing employee training program** that emphasizes the employee's responsibility for system security. User error or misjudgment are the top ways risks are introduced into a network. Embed the message in policies, job descriptions, new hire training, company meetings, newsletter briefings, and general company communications. You can't say it enough. Make it part of your remote work company culture.
2. **Provide firewall security** for your company internet connection. Firewall technology has changed a lot. Make sure your firewall security accommodates internal firewalls, traditional VPNs, and new cloud technology e.g., RAP networks based on your business needs and the geographic spread of the team.
3. **Automate software updates** for operating systems and apps on all business devices including mobile devices.
4. **Automate business data and system information backup process** on all business devices including mobile devices.

5. **Secure Wi-Fi networks** by hiding the service set identifier (SSID). Turn on encryption so a password is required for network access and educate your end users about password security.
6. **Create individual accounts for each employee or approved user e.g., contractors, consultants, or vendor partners**, then audit the system regularly and purge inactive accounts.
7. **Articulate clear policies regarding non-approved software installations on business devices.** Incorporate these policies into your employee training programs and reiterate the message often.
8. **Build a password maintenance program that emphasizes password protection practices and the need for routine password updates.** Incorporate them into your employee training programs and build it into your calendar to send out reminders periodically throughout the year.

Legal, Compliance, and Regulatory Considerations

The year 2020 highlighted the disconnect in employment law, regulatory practices, IT and data security, and a remote workforce. Workplace changes happened so fast they were far ahead of legislation, particularly in the US. Take time to familiarize yourself with what's happening with labor laws, employee tax requirements, employee privacy, data privacy, and OSHA regulations in your areas of operation and incorporate them into your remote work plan. Research your tax obligations and employer registration requirements in the states that your remote employees reside. Stay informed. As I am writing this, we are at the beginning of a period of chaos. At this moment, courts seem reluctant to comment on issues related to remote work. In 2021, New Hampshire sued Massachusetts (*State of New Hampshire vs. Commonwealth of Massachusetts*) claiming New Hampshire remote work residents should not have to pay Massachusetts income tax when they were employed by Massachusetts companies but working full time at their NH homes. The US Supreme Court rejected the case without comment. Given the rapid rise in employee demands for flexible work options and the effects of tight labor markets, I anticipate we are at the beginning of what promises to be an ongoing, complex legal examination of the definition of work, the workplace, and employment.

When I consulted my employment law colleagues while researching this chapter, they emphasized the need for consistent practices, attention to fundamentals, and constant vigilance. I'll discuss this in more detail in Chapter 6 when I cover talent management systems and the employee lifecycle. Here I will say, stay consistent and follow current labor laws by state and maintain good labor practices in your employee relations, compensation, benefits, and

HR systems. Keep excellent work records and build remote work policies and job descriptions that spell out work expectations then align them with current labor laws, both state and federal. In Chapter 4, I discuss the need to establish operating protocols that define work expectations for your remote employees to hedge against discrimination or equity concerns. In Chapter 5, I discuss work performance accountability measures that provide consistency and parity. Take the key points from each of these chapters and incorporate them into your operating framework for your remote work plan after you vet them against current employment law at the moment you make your plan. Apply everything consistently across your workforce regardless of work location. As with our infrastructure discussion earlier in this chapter, I urge you to cultivate relationships with subject matter experts you can trust. I, myself, maintain contacts with skilled employment lawyers, compliance specialists, HR leaders, and professional organizations in these fields so I can consult with them on critical remote work issues. I work hard to keep my clients updated on these topics as well as changes occur.

If your employees use their personal devices for work, be extra careful. Having employees use personal devices is not unusual these days but it does elevate the risk. Business apps on personal devices still need to be maintained, synced, and updated regularly. Since the device is privately owned, it means there will be other apps on it that aren't business related. To reduce business concerns, you still need business data backed up, regular operating system updates, and all apps updated regularly on these devices. Have your employees sign a non-disclosure agreement stating your policy for data and information sharing so you have something on record in the event the employee leaves. Think through your policies related to a lost or stolen personal device.

Those policies need to be explicitly communicated to your employee up front so there are no surprises. Remotely tracking a lost business device or wiping a stolen business device's hard drive is one thing, tracking a personal device or wiping personal information off someone's personal property may have very different legal implications depending on where the device is located geographically. Besides devices, remote employees could have access to data, information, company systems, and intellectual property. We have all our employees sign a simple non-disclosure and privacy agreement indicating their understanding that all this belongs to the company. We keep a copy, and we give the employee a copy. We also have a simple checklist for the termination process that address the steps we take for voluntary and involuntary employee terminations so we can shut off access appropriately. We review this checklist with the key stakeholders e.g., our technical team, HR, and operations so file transfers, system access, email, etc. so everyone knows what to do if someone leaves.

Role of the Help Desk

I've mentioned remote employee end user training a lot throughout this chapter. All my CIO and technology colleagues that have internal help desk teams have mentioned the help desk's value as a training resource for the company's remote system end-users. Remote employees, regardless of their job title, need, at minimum, a basic understanding of IT fundamentals – modem, router, the role of the internet service providers (ISP), use of secure hot spots, device operating systems, video conferencing functionality, tech security, etc. It's a pretty long list. Most of the time, remote employees must troubleshoot their technology themselves and with fundamental technical knowledge can take care of 90% of their own problems. Teaching your remote employees IT basics will have a positive impact on that employee's productivity. In Chapter 7, I'll discuss remote workforce training and I'll address this in more detail. But rethinking the role of the help desk and utilizing them proactively as tech educators, advisers, and service providers rather than just tech "fixers" can help remote teams in a lot of interesting ways. Help desk employees deal with their remote end users remotely, so help desk employees are experienced remote work professionals themselves. Today's technology tools allow your help desk staff to remote access devices and evaluate, troubleshoot, diagnose, fix, update, backup, locate, and wipe devices from afar. But your help desk team can also teach their remote colleagues how to problem solve on their own and build accessible learning content so remote employees can reference a solution for a typical device problem in real time. Internal IT help desk team members are uniquely positioned to play this role and provide support, training, and real time troubleshooting advice. They have technical knowledge, and they see the impacts of poor remote employee user practices firsthand. They can detect user trends and system challenges faster because they are in contact with multiple remote users. The help desk team knows what's normal and what's not. When help desk team members are company employees, they have access to technical knowledge of the company's business goals, business systems, operating systems, security practices, and business devices. They can troubleshoot at a system level, then proactively reach out to their remote colleagues, discuss fixes, host tutorials, and provide online resources.

This is the compelling business case for maintaining an in-house help desk for small to midsize companies. However, given the nature of technology today, the changes in our approach to technical infrastructure, the adoption of cloud computing, and cyber-security concerns, if you do choose an internal help desk team, I recommend you redesign their role, so it includes more teaching capabilities, service delivery, and proactive intervention. Help desk employees can contribute more than security training and end user support. One example of this is a client of mine, Amy C. Amy works at a US-based consumer insurance company with 4,000 employees spread across the US. She was the company expert on remote work. In 2020, when the company sent most of its employees home, Amy recruited the company help desk to assist with her company-wide remote work plan implementation. Amy turned the help desk team into remote work "super users" and enlisted them as active change agents supporting the remote work rollout. She made them part of the rollout team, enlisted them to do remote work IT security training, and had them teaching basic technology troubleshooting skills to 4,000 first time remote employees. This team had an active voice in the rollout process. Things went smoother, resulting in higher productivity, less business disruption, and lower stress for everyone.

I know maintaining an internal help desk goes against current business trends and adding non-revenue generating headcount is a hard sell at most companies these days. IT departments have been shrinking for years and choosing more cost-conscious, flexible options has been the default choice. With remote teams, this may or may not be the best model. I think there is a strong business case to be made for re-thinking the role of the help desk and using it more strategically to accelerate productivity and proactively manage security when you adopt remote work operating models. Consider investing in a specialized in-house IT team of capable generalists who aren't just "fixers" but rather focus on teaching, mentoring, supporting, and nurturing your remote workforce. Train them to be technology educators to support rollouts, system upgrades, new tool trends, etc. so you have a dedicated resource with inside business knowledge and passion for your mission. At minimum, you need a smart, strategic IT executive who sees the big picture along with a collaborative cybersecurity expert who can stay abreast of security trends. They must work together in lockstep with your operations team to keep things running smoothly and securely. They also need to stay on top of your third-party vendors to keep them honest and ensure you get what you pay for in your service contracts.

If you do decide to maintain an internal team, structure the job requirements to fit the needs of this new remote work help desk structure. Just as the role of network administration has changed, shift the help desk role so this team provides maximum value to your remote workforce and aligns with your business goals. Review the competencies and skill requirements and upgrade the job descriptions and job expectations accordingly. If you elect to hire third-party vendors or contractors, negotiate for robust, high-touch end user support services rather than evaluating a vendor strictly on bargain-basement price. If you decide to outsource your help desk entirely, push to have a dedicated help desk team that learns your organization's systems and practices, so they are a more useful resource to your people. If you are automating your help desk, going self-serve, or using a third-party outsource solution, you will have to devise an alternate plan for end user IT security and IT fundamentals training for your remote employees.

Business Continuity and Disaster Recovery Planning Post-2020

Adopting a remote work strategy has built in advantages for business continuity and disaster recovery planning. Remote work means less work disruption in the event of many emergencies. If the internet or cell service is available, and the remote work infrastructure is in place, work can continue in remote teams with minimal disruption. The process of adopting a remote work strategy presents a perfect opportunity to review your current business continuity and disaster recovery plans post-2020 to ensure everything is aligned. Defining roles and responsibilities, planning work processes and workflows, identifying risks and vulnerabilities, and workforce training are all fundamentals of business continuity planning, so, you get double the value for your planning efforts. Same thing with disaster recovery planning. As you develop your remote work strategy, consider how you will maintain your operations in good times and in bad.

If business continuity is the process of keeping your business going under any circumstances, disaster recovery is about contingency planning for your infrastructure in troubled times. That means developing a comprehensive inventory of your remote work infrastructure assets, a contact list with defined roles and responsibilities, your communication strategy, and a contingency plan for your service providers so you have a gameplan in place in the event of an emergency. Make sure your team has access to the plan under all circumstances. Keeping it in binders in a file cabinet or in local digital files only accessible with VPN access isn't helpful. Disaster recovery plans are about proactively safeguarding your systems, data, and records; enabling operations to continue during and after the disaster; minimizing the recovery time; and establishing agreement on emergency practices across the organization so everyone stays in sync. Think through the "what-ifs" carefully. Since disasters tend to be geographically specific, having a remote team means you can shift the workload from one regional team to another regional team that is fully operational. Since remote employees are highly digital, you can reroute work processes through other channels if one system is interrupted. Remote teams are ultra-dependent on technology. You need the ability to distribute messages to the entire group quickly and email isn't the most efficient channel for this purpose. Build emergency text broadcast capabilities into your plan. Happily, there are a lot of group messaging software tools available today that help you reach everyone in your organization almost instantly via voicemail or text.

While I'm discussing these tools in the context of emergencies, I'd also like to point out that I've experimented using these push text messaging platforms for other purposes beyond crisis communications. In several cases, we used push text messaging strategically for remote team training or change management messaging. In one instance, I helped a large university roll out a very sophisticated facilities maintenance system that was highly dependent on smartphones. Many of the existing facilities team worked remotely but had little experience with smart phone technology (hard to believe today, but true). Few employees had used text messaging prior to this program rollout. Once everyone received their new cell phones during the rollout, we needed a clever way to get them engaged with their new devices. We created a fun text messaging game that allowed employees to win small prizes if they responded via text to our push text messages. We saw team members helping each other through the process and learning the technology through hands on use. We learned a valuable lesson, don't assume everyone is tech savvy or uses technology the same way you do. Happily, this implementation improved everyone's skills so future emergency messages are more likely to reach their intended target. When you create continuity or disaster recovery plans, test them beforehand so you can identify problems ahead of time and fix them before an emergency occurs.

Highlights

Remote work infrastructure is foundational to your remote work operating model as it's the infrastructure that provides the technical scaffold that allows your remote team to connect and get work done. The following elements are vital considerations to ensure your employees can stay in touch and do their jobs while also protecting your company.

Networks, the cloud, and business systems access

- Remote teams are dependent on technical infrastructure to get work done, communicate, and stay connected with you and their team.
- Infrastructure today depends on the cloud and Wi-Fi networks.
- Advances in network technology allow for flexibility and are much more dependent on third-party vendors.
- Build a network that suits your business and is easy to scale.
- Ensure your network solution provides consistent, reliable access so your remote employees can get work done efficiently.
- Focus on end-to-end system interoperability.
- Consult your end users and include them in the design, implementation, and test process to ensure the final product functions as intended.

Devices, apps, and backups

- Devices are lighter, more powerful, and more mobile than ever.
- Devices can be stolen, lost, broken, and hacked – prepare for these scenarios and have plans in place to address problems quickly.
- Have an update and backup plan that includes cell phones, apps, and any additional device used for work purposes.

Systems, data, and IP security

- It is no longer a question of if, but when you will have a breach. Plan for the worst in advance.
- Provide an ongoing employee training program that emphasizes the employee's responsibility for system security.
- Provide firewall security for your company internet connection.
- Automate software updates for operating systems and apps on all business devices including mobile devices.
- Automate business data and system information backup process on all business devices including mobile devices.
- Secure Wi-Fi networks by hiding the SSID.
- Create individual accounts for each employee or approved user e.g., contractors, consultants, or vendor partners, then audit the system regularly and purge inactive accounts.
- Articulate clear policies regarding non-approved software installations on business devices.
- Build a password maintenance program that emphasizes password protection practices and the need for routine password updates.
- Balance security with operational productivity. Your systems can't be locked down so tight that remote employees are unable to meet their job requirements.

Legal, compliance, regulatory considerations

- Legal definitions of work, the workplace, and employment are changing and will continue to evolve.
- Partner with trusted experts to ensure you stay on top of ongoing legal discussions, litigation, and legislation.
- Stay proactive and aware as things are shifting quickly.

Role of the help desk

- The help desk role has evolved dramatically.
- Help desk professionals today must be more proactive, customer-service oriented, consultative, and ready to teach, mentor, and coach their end users.
- Help desk professionals, like remote employees, must continually upgrade their skills to stay relevant as new technologies emerge.
- When using third-party vendors for help desk support, evaluate their effectiveness on their service delivery rather than price.

Business continuity and disaster recovery planning post-2020

- Adopting a remote work strategy has built in business continuity and disaster recovery advantages.
- Practice the plans in advance of any incident and keep plan information virtually accessible to key stakeholders in the process.
- Don't assume everyone is tech savvy, test your plan to observe their effectiveness and adjust them accordingly so they are ready when you need them.

Chapter 5

Component Two: Operational Protocols

Technical infrastructure is the first step as it, among other things, enables technical connectivity between business systems and the team. It's foundational for facilitating remote work. Operational protocols are equally important as they will dictate how remote employees will get work done within the infrastructure you build. Design your infrastructure and operational protocols simultaneously so they work in harmony rather than at odds with each other. If your business infrastructure and operational protocols are not in sync, it will be hard for your employees to complete their daily tasks and work output will suffer. I can't stress this enough, the interaction between these two components has a major impact on work productivity and team burnout. You will have ongoing problems and add costly stress on your teams if the two are out of sync. This is one more reason why multi-discipline coalitions are a necessity from day one and why a holistic, collaborative, multi-discipline approach to operationalizing remote work programs yields better results.

Operational protocols define:

- functional requirements of work tasks,
- team communication protocols,
- work schedules and defining availability,
- software and business system use,
- security responsibilities,
- workplace safety.

DOI: 10.4324/9781003243557-5

Work Processes and Workflows

Work processes and workflows define the way work gets done and dictate the functional steps it takes to complete them successfully. Defining work processes and workflows early on helps each team member determine their deliverables, learn how their efforts contribute value, and highlights how an individual team member's work impacts their peers. For a remote team, working from multiple locations, this gives everyone a sense of their place in the team, provides work structure, and provides a sort of "virtual" office space. They are necessary for measuring work performance as well. I'll talk about this in more detail in Chapter 5 when I discuss measuring work performance and employee accountability. Work processes and workflows are individual to specific job roles but have distinct characteristics dictated by the type of work involved. Routine, repeatable tasks are transactional and more prescribed, they depend on timelines and proper execution of steps. Problem-solving, analytics, and creative thinking tasks are more outcomes driven and depend more on defined project objectives, project timelines, and agreed upon deliverables.

Transactional, prescribed work processes and workflows are usually related to a fixed business process that requires consistent, regulated execution. Deviation from the established process is a problem as accuracy, timeliness of execution, and reliability are critical. These types of work tasks are highly defined and tightly scripted for a specific reason. They might be tied to calendar deadlines such as finance or accounting roles or they may be driven by mandates of one kind or another e.g., legal, compliance, safety, security, technical or functional system requirements, etc. For these types of repetitive, sequential work tasks, you want predictable adherence rather than creativity as the process or workflow requirements dictate the necessary steps. Documenting these types of process and workflows is straightforward if a bit tedious and time consuming initially. It's more about accuracy, process adherence, and noting the reasons why it's important to stick to the process so employees understand the "why" behind the task. When these types of jobs go remote for the first time, the biggest hurdle is a lack of accurate documentation that outlines the full workflow. Often, knowledge of these work processes resides in someone's head.

Traditionally, transactional knowledge is passed from employee to employee the old-fashioned way – someone sits next to you, looks over your shoulder, and tells you what button to push. You take notes and then ask questions of the more experienced person sitting next to you when you run into a problem. Mentoring is done in real time, face-to-face. In remote teams, this isn't practical. Going remote with these roles requires a thorough review of the current work processes to ensure each step is accurately recorded, still relevant, and business necessary. Use your functional experts to help document the specific steps in sequential order. Add visuals whenever you can. There are lots of different ways to do this – through shared file tools, wiki discussion boards, via recorded video, visual screenshots, screen sharing, etc. This is not a printed document as remote workflows will shift as technology continues to evolve and new employees with new skills and experience join the team. As you document the process, evaluate each step to ensure it is still relevant and useful in a remote work environment. Use tools that allow for dynamic, real-time updates and keep master documents in an accessible, shared place online to avoid problems with version control. As with any record keeping, assign someone responsibility for maintaining these masters so they stay up to date and to drive continued productivity, build in reminders into your plan to conduct periodic assessments to ensure the processes are still relevant and necessary over time. Add a context for each functional step as it helps the remote employee understand the business rationale and the consequences of non-compliance then develop a new hire training process so new remote employees are set up for success. NOTE: The repetitiveness combined with the need for accuracy and regularity make these tasks prime candidates for automation and/or consolidation to achieve more predictability and control. Consider this as you build your plan.

Work processes and workflows for knowledge workers who must think critically, self-organize, and problem solve solutions serve an entirely different purpose. Defining and documenting work processes and workflows for these types of roles will depend on organizational objectives, the team objectives, team interdependencies, project phases, and desired business outcome rather than dictated, prescribed steps. Get your team involved with designing them so you have a better chance of gaining employee buy-in. These types of work processes are more general, less procedural. They focus on things like team roles and responsibilities, collaboration and interaction protocols, and interdependencies e.g., product development, software development, data analysis, engineering design, etc. Avoid getting too prescriptive with the "how" as that will start to feel like micromanagement to these employees. The employee won't like being told how to do the job, and they'll feel patronized or perceive these types of dictates as a lack of trust. This is counterproductive for team productivity and team cohesion and wears away morale. Seeking employee input promotes more innovative solutions and keeps people's energy high as whatever approach gets adopted comes from them. Remote employees in these roles still need some definition and a shared knowledge of interdependencies so collaboration runs smoothly, and everyone learns how to work together toward a shared goal as one cohesive, engaged team.

Communication Protocols

Communication protocols are serious business for remote teams. Don't cut corners here. Effective communication between humans is tricky under any circumstances, even face-to-face teams experience communication challenges. In remote teams, the dependency on digital channels, the speed of interaction, the 24×7 availability pressure, and the shifting way people now define connection are changing how we define interactions and, in some cases, even rewiring our brains. New communication technologies give us a lot of business advantages. They certainly support and enable remote teamwork in new, exciting, and innovative ways. But the digitization of communications mixed with the different generational uses of technology has disrupted the way we interact with each other to do that work. Communication is dispersed and multi-channel now. Work processes can happen in real time across time zones, synchronously, or asynchronously. We are used to thinking of communication as a feedback loop. I convey information to you; you receive it and respond back. Traditionally this has been a closed-loop cycle. But not anymore. Today we interact with work colleagues differently, weaving online contact and offline contact into ongoing communication threads that can extend forever. Highly effective when handled thoughtfully and executed with purpose. I call this the O2O2O effect (online to offline to online) – a continuous flow. I'll cover this in more detail in Chapter 11. When leveraged correctly this O2O2O approach is great for building team engagement, encouraging trust, and supporting camaraderie. However, there are so many channels to choose from that it can get very confusing amazingly fast. Operational chaos will ensue without an agreed upon communication structure.

When digital channels require channel access, functional tool knowledge, and internet connectivity; team communication protocols can't be left to chance. Nor can they be left up to individual preference. Digital channels create an open loop communication dynamic that can deceive users into thinking they are efficient and productive because of the volume of communications they can send in a workday. But this doesn't mean we're effective. As an individual, I can use my preferred device to rapidly send lots of emails, texts, IMs, and voicemails. But speed and technical capabilities are not the problem. If my intended audience for my messages isn't connected to the same channels as me, if all my emails are blocked by spam filters, or if the intended message recipient fails to open my messages for any reason, then the only person I'm talking to is myself. I'm not communicating to anyone because no one on the receiving end is receiving. Communication doesn't occur until the recipient receives the message, opens it, and responds. If every team member chooses their own channels based on their own preferences, that's when breakdowns happen, and things can get ugly fast. Getting the team involved in the development of communication protocols connects the protocol users with the operational results and helps bring awareness and highlights the problems with non-compliance.

For a communication protocol to work, three things need to occur:

1. All team members need consistent technical access to the agreed upon communication tools,
2. There must be shared agreement on each tool's use,
3. Everyone needs to commit to adopt and use the tools as intended.

As driving tool adoption is a top priority, I recommend you start out using as many existing tools as you can to minimize impacts on the current work process. Then gradually add new tools over time as the business dictates or critical operational pain points emerge. If you do decide to adopt new tools, I recommend you pilot them with a small select group before you do a full team rollout. Choose a variety of test users. Include early adopters and reasonable skeptics so you can get a fair assessment. Evaluate the tool's productivity impacts and weigh the pros and cons against the criticality of your business needs. When you evaluate the product in test, ask yourself lots of user-based questions: Does the tool make work easier, add value in critical ways, is it cost-effective, are there hidden fees, can my least technical team member navigate it, what are the technical requirements to run it, are there security concerns, can every team member access it in their work location? If you choose to adopt something new, plan for a certain amount of operational disruption in advance. Build in plans for training, follow the change management plan I discuss in Chapter 9 and then commit to use the tool for at least six months to a year to give it a fair chance. Once you and the team adopt a tool, be a visible role model. If you use it, it's more likely others will, too.

Work Schedules and Defining Availability

Remote team scheduling and remote employee availability are hot topics for a variety of reasons. First, it's a key indicator executives, managers, and co-workers often use to judge performance and individual team member dedication. We'll talk about the pros and cons of this in the chapter. Second, it's the number one reason remote employees burn out, especially in international teams. They overwork and feel unable to unplug if they fail to negotiate availability boundaries right away and because they are conscientious, they try to remain available at all hours. Third, building a team scheduling template helps you determine staffing requirements that are appropriate for the workload and realistically evaluate the level of coverage required to get a job done right. Dedicated remote employees without clear boundaries often feel they are obligated to be available 24×7, if that happens, the rest of the team gets used to this standard and gets impatient when the team member tries to step away for a break. The remote team member experiences a high degree of stress as they are convinced, they are letting people down if they miss a message or detach from their device. Because the remote employee works out of your line of sight, they will silently burnout and you won't even know it.

When you lead a remote team, you need to account for different time zones and create a scheduling and availability standard that is fair to everyone. Defining the schedule and setting availability boundaries is step one. Step two is helping people stick to the agreed upon availability by checking in periodically and reassuring people it's ok to keep the agreed upon schedule. Pay close attention to your new team members as they will feel additional pressure to impress. Step three is checking in with the whole team to make sure there is no scope creep, and the schedule is adequately covered for the workload. Check yourself as well. Your emails and other messaging sent during off hours puts pressure on your team to do the same unless your behavior is part of the agreement. Even then, appreciate it's hard to ignore your boss. Be a good role model and maintain a healthy schedule. I've had more than one remote professional ask my advice on the best ways to negotiate healthy boundaries with their boss and their co-workers.

In one case, I met a young, exceptionally talented project manager working for an international engineering firm who was completely exhausted. The teams she supported expected her to be available 24×7 (or at least she thought they did). Over a two-year period, her global colleagues failed to consciously recognize the number of time zones they occupied. It simply never occurred to them that time zone fatigue was a factor because it wasn't a stated consideration for the group. People just sucked it up and got on with things. As a result, the project manager was reluctant to speak up because she needed her job, and she didn't want to disappoint anyone or appear unable to manage her work responsibilities. Since her boss never discussed availability expectations, she failed to raise the issue. Often her boss was the person who imposed on her the most. In the end, I encouraged her to speak up and raise the issue with her boss and her team. Both were shocked to learn just how close she was to collapse as it had never occurred to them anything was wrong. In the end, the team hired several additional project managers across the globe so work could continue, and the young project manager could get some rest.

Scheduling and availability protocols must include provisions for business meetings as well. It's too easy to overwhelm the team with back-to-back online meetings that take up so much of the day that remote employees can't get their work done. Screen fatigue is real. Create a meeting format that builds in breaks. Many of my clients have implemented "no-meeting" days and in my team, if one of my remote employees indicates they are right in the middle of something, we push the meeting to a new time. Use your calendar tools thoughtfully, learn their functionality, and set the calendar invitation defaults to 30 minutes or 45 minutes rather than a full hour. I recommend keeping meetings as short as possible 20–30 minutes maximum. When the work is done, don't linger. I give my people permission to evaluate a meeting invitation, question its business purpose, and decline the meeting if it makes good business sense to do so. Make it ok for everyone to block out time in their calendars for work time and respite breaks. Meetings are an important touch point in remote teams and a necessary business tool, but meetings can get out of hand if you don't determine the format, train the team how to run an effective meeting, and then hold yourself and the team accountable to the agreed upon meeting protocols.

Software and Business Systems

Remote teams are dependent on technology for just about every aspect of remote work. When you adopt remote work as a business strategy, your number one priority is to make sure your people have the technical capability to access any business systems safely and securely so they can reliably get their job done. System access, work process, and team communications always conflict with system and data security. To keep things safe, business systems and communication channels need to be locked down. If systems are too locked down, it makes system access clunky, isolates remote employees, and slows down work. To achieve optimal remote team productivity, you must find a balance between these things. Get your Operations, Security, and IT leaders together to figure out the right balance as a team. This is critically important – if things are clunky and slow, employees will find ways to solve the problem by introducing their own workarounds. Ironically, these workarounds often introduce the very risk your security protocols are set up to avoid. By tackling the problem at the system level, involving your multi-disciplinary coalitions, and then monitoring the remote employees responsible for completing work tasks using those systems to identify pain points, you can avoid a lot of future headaches.

Besides systems access, there are all the ancillary tools remote teams need for file sharing, video or audio conferencing, team engagement, chatting, collaboration, etc. Before you buy lots of new tools, make sure you evaluate what you already own. Conduct an audit of existing tools. Measure their functional capabilities against your new remote work protocols and survey your teams to determine what they are currently using and what gaps exist. Are the existing tools a help or a hindrance? Tools that offer multifunctionality, and centralize access like Microsoft Teams, Slack, Asana, Basecamp, and Monday.com (to name just a few) are now widely available and very appealing because they provide one central workspace that helps aggregate work tasks and team interactions in one place. Today's tools are cloud-based for easy online access. Each of these platforms has pros and cons with affordable options for any size business. These tools routinely add additional functionality and may have features that fit your needs but are going unused because the functionality was added after you adopted the tool. You may find that the very function you need is already available. All you need to do is train your employees how to use it.

Remote Workforce and System User Security Responsibilities

It's no secret that cyber-attacks are on the rise. It doesn't matter what is the size of your organization, what devices you use, or what type of infrastructure you construct; it's not "if," but "when" something will happen these days. As I mentioned earlier, technology users and lack of system maintenance cause most security breaches and you will have to balance system security and work productivity. Lock down too much and no one can get work done. Your best option according to my CIO friends is vigilance, user training, and constant messaging to users that reinforces the importance of cyber security. Use your help desk strategically but embed security into your culture. Don't cut corners on this. Work with your remote work coalitions to make training a standard for all levels of the organization whether you are a small organization or a large one.

This must extend to everyone in your work ecosystem. When your team works remotely, you have a lot of people accessing your systems through multiple devices – leaders, employees, contractors, temps, interns, third-party vendors, and customers. Anyone who touches your systems, with whom you interact online, or with whom you collaborate is a potential point of security failure. Everyone who has system access of any kind needs some sort of training, so they are alert to their responsibilities. Messaging related to cybersecurity must be a part of your onboarding process, noted in your employee policies, vendor agreements, contractor contracts, and reinforced by new hire trainers and your help desk. For customers and all third-party vendors with system access, you can build it into your user agreements, insert it into your contracts, or add it to your privacy disclaimers.

Remote Workplace Safety

There is a lot of discussion around this topic. I have a small team and we're unable to assume the cost of expensive equipment for every employee. Yet my team's well-being is important to me, so I make every effort possible to educate my people on safe work practices and adopting a healthy lifestyle. But I think we must elevate the conversation about workplace safety beyond who is going to pay for an office chair to think more broadly about workplace safety. As far as I can tell, humans have wrestled with ergonomics as long as we've used tools. The formal study of ergonomics started at the beginning of the industrial revolution as a framework for designing machinery that improved manufacturing productivity. Today we look at ergonomics in the context of repetitive tasks, stand-up desks, and how much time we spend sitting while we stare at an electronic screen.

But the issue of remote workplace safety is broader and more comprehensive than office equipment and screen time. As remote work grows, we need to re-evaluate and re-define everyone's role and responsibility in this new, evolving workplace through public debate and workplace experimentation. How are we defining workplace safety as a society as remote work continues to grow? In addition to physical well-being, how do we address the mental health of our employees who work out of our sight? Who is responsible for what in this new context where so much of a remote employee's work experience is self-determined? Home office design, remote work product design, work process, system access, evolving technology, individual workplace set-ups, employee participation in remote work, social connection, employer responsibility, leadership techniques, and even the definition of what constitutes a healthy workday schedule for remote work need to be discussed and examined. All are contributing factors to operational productivity, workplace safety, team engagement, and overall employee satisfaction. Who is liable for what and what is or is not acceptable remote work practice is currently an open debate.

From a practical perspective, as a business owner running a fully remote company, I'm doing what I can to educate myself and my people, remain vigilant on changes as they arise, continue to open discussions with my people and my colleagues, and cultivate strategic partnerships with subject matter experts in employment law, compliance, mental health, and workplace safety. I advise you to do the same. The other thing I'm doing is standardizing remote work practices based on thousands of discussions with remote professionals, my own operational experience, and best practice research so I have a clear structure in place for measuring, tracking, and continual improvement. My goal is to proactively shape this future as much as I can. On a day-to-day basis, I monitor team productivity and team well-being to make sure my team and I can meet our current business obligations, I actively strive to create a healthy team culture, while working toward our longer-term business growth plans. This means I am constantly monitoring the systems and protocols we've adopted to ensure they are still relevant and sufficient. That they are working for us rather than against us. As this is an evolving landscape, these check-ins are necessary to maintain a continually productive remote work business model and I recommend you build this practice into your long-term maintenance plans as well.

Highlights

If infrastructure provides the technical scaffold that supports connectivity, access, and security; business protocols define the rules of operation that keep your remote team in sync. They are the basis for your virtual workplace and set the stage for the development of meaningful performance metrics making accountability possible. The operating protocols most critical for remote team success include:

Work processes and workflows

- Infrastructure provides the technical framework that enables remote work.
- Remote work operational protocols dictate how work gets done.
- Routine, repeatable tasks yield more predictable process steps that depend on consistent execution and process compliance.
- Critical thinking functions require workflows more dependent on agreed upon outcomes, deliverables, and timelines as how the work gets done is less critical.

Communication protocols

- Communication today has changed rapidly due to technological advances.
- How we connect and build relationships is more fluid – moving from online contact to in-person, offline contact in what I call an extended O2O2O feedback chain.
- Different generations use digital communications differently and with so many channels to choose from, there needs to be team agreement as to what tools the team will use for what purpose.
- For a communication protocol to work, three things need to occur:
  - All team members need consistent technical access to the agreed upon communication tools,
  - There must be shared agreement on each tool's use,
  - Everyone needs to commit to adopt and use the tools as intended.

Work schedules and defining availability

- As availability is a primary metric used to evaluate work performance, setting parameters early in a remote team is crucial for everyone's peace of mind and well-being.

- Check in with the team periodically to avoid scope creep and to assure team members that agreed upon availability will be honored.
- Build a team staffing schedule that considers time zones within international teams and be explicit about availability expectations.
- Be a good role model so your employees don't feel the pressure to be instantly available in response to your requests and messages.

Software and business systems

- When you adopt a remote work operating model, your priority is to ensure your employees have full access to the business systems necessary for them to do their jobs.
- There is always a tension between system access and security that you must navigate carefully to keep systems safe while enabling employees to achieve the desired work productivity.
- Security and operations need to work in partnership to achieve a reasonable balance between the two.

Remote workforce and system user security responsibilities

- Cyber-attacks are on the rise and will continue to accelerate as our dependence on technology grows.
- Device users are the biggest security weakness.
- Build user security into the fabric of all your employee training, make it a part of your culture to be on the lookout, and continue to communicate consistently to keep the issue top of mind.
- For customers and third-party vendors build it into your user agreements, insert it into your contracts, or add it to your privacy disclaimers.

Remote workplace safety

- It's a bigger discussion than ergonomics and all of us need to work together to define and shape the workplace of the future.
- Partner with experts in multiple disciplines like employment law, compliance, mental health, and other aspects of workplace safety to stay on top of changes and to contribute to the discussion.

Chapter 6

Component Three: Performance Accountability Measures

There is a pervasive myth that remote work is an excuse for screwing off. If I sound a little cranky about this, I am. This persistent attitude is insulting to remote professionals everywhere who, for years, have contributed business value daily regardless of their work location. Remote work is a legitimate and productive practice when executed deliberately and strategically. This negative attitude about remote work is particularly insulting to anyone who successfully and productively worked from home during 2020. Despite a complete lack of social support and little professional preparation other than "don't come back to the office, figure out how to make it work," a significant percentage of first-time remote workers did figure it out. They kept their companies afloat by showing up for work and doing their job every day. Remote employees as a group have always delivered. Yes, there will always be some individuals who don't perform up to standard, but there are non-performers at the office. Non-performance is not unique or specific to remote work. Some people simply fail to perform regardless of their work location. Yet remote employees have consistently been held to a higher standard than traditional office workers. We are penalized for working outside the typical office or away from the "home office" just because we're remote. Our business contributions, considerable skills, and self-reliance have gone unacknowledged and largely dismissed for years.

In my remote experience it's been harder to hide poor performance as a remote professional because dependability and work delivery are such a core part of a remote employee's job, whereas showing up at the office and looking busy is given a free pass. I say all this because this chapter addresses performance accountability in the context of remote teams. If you want your team to perform, you must set them up for success and hold them accountable through active management and mindful leadership. This transcends work location. Stop blaming remote work and start examining your approach and your biases. Happily, any of the techniques I discuss, when applied as outlined, will improve performance accountability for in-person employees as well as your remote employees. That's important for any of you managing hybrid remote teams with some employees working in offices and some not. Apply these systems consistently without regard to work location and take note of your results. I think you'll be surprised to see productivity gains across the board. What's the old saying? "What gets measured, gets done." Providing clear expectations up front, then holding yourself, your managers, supervisors, and employees accountable may seem like a too obvious solution. I'm not saying this straightforward approach is simple or easy when applied in real life. Nothing is simple whenever people are involved because people are hard to lead or manage because they are so messy. Even executing on a simple solution gets more complicated because people's behavior is variable. Humans are many things, including emotional, illogical, and sometimes uncooperative.

Holding employees accountable is one of the most important parts of a leader's job. Yet the reality is many leaders aren't good at holding employees accountable nor are they good at linking job performance to measurable criteria regardless of where that employee sits. Many business leaders delude themselves into thinking that they have effective metrics for measuring in-person employees. They also presume physical presence is synonymous with productivity and performance execution. But when I work with clients and dig below the surface to examine those supposedly existing metrics, I discover most companies don't have clear measures. This dependence on physical presence hides an ugly truth. Most managers can't manage team productivity because they don't know how to do it and keeping everyone in an office, so you have physical proximity is a poor substitute for judging performance effectiveness. Let's stop fooling ourselves. Non-performers exist in every organization and a good many of them work in offices. Blaming non-productivity or perceived non-performance strictly on remote work isn't accurate nor is it fair. It's time to change the game for all employees and adopt metrics that are meaningful, and business focused. Then we need to teach leaders, managers, and supervisors how to apply those metrics systematically with deliberate precision so we can create standard performance accountability across the entire workforce fairly and equitably.

As you continue to build out your remote work plan, appreciate this component, performance accountability, is the key to business success as it dictates team productivity by requiring leaders to shift from cops to coaches and enabling them with the skills to manage job performance through mentoring and coaching rather than command, control, and micromanagement. While the leader plays a significant role, remote employees have responsibilities, too. To fully realize everyone's potential, every team member – from executive to line employee – must own their piece of the puzzle. In previous chapters, we set up infrastructure and workplace protocols to enable remote work. In this chapter, we focus on work execution and the process for evaluating a remote employee's performance success and failure. To be fair and meaningful, any effective performance accountability system requires measurability against some baseline such as job requirements, or defined business goals. In this chapter, I've broken these criteria into the following categories:

- organizational mission and core values
- business goals and deliverables
- universally defined performance metrics
- job descriptions
- functional requirements and existing KPIs
- interpersonal interaction protocols
- meeting protocols

Organizational Mission and Core Values

A lot of people ask me about building remote team culture, remote team engagement, and improving remote employee retention. I always say the same thing – it's all about setting expectations up front, then inserting touch points throughout the entire talent lifecycle to observe and provide feedback, while infusing your culture into everything you do. This is something that I'll discuss in this chapter with continued discussion in Chapter 7. Institutionalizing a culture starts with the story we business owners and executive leaders tell our people. This includes who we are, why we exist, and what we value as an organization. Ultimately, it's what we stand for as a business. Defining the attributes of your mission and core values allows you to define the behaviors you and your leaders will hold yourselves and your employees to as part of your accountability criteria. Yes, performance accountability needs to be rooted in job performance, business delivery, and results; however, culture is all about the vibe you're trying to create to get people energized and proud to be a part of the team, so they perform well, take pride in their role, and make a choice to stay. For many people today this stems from something bigger than just business goals and work deliverables, they want to know their hard work is meaningful, that it matters.

At Sophaya, we keep it simple. Our mission is to help our clients successfully operationalize remote work programs and optimize remote team productivity. We do this by helping our clients deploy standardized remote work best practices and providing remote work professional certifications and remote work business skills training at our Remote Nation Institute (RNI). Everything we do as a team supports this mission. Our vision is to help every client and every member of the remote workforce achieve the full value of remote work. Our performance expectations and accountability systems align with this mission and vision. Anyone joining the team is expected to be a champion for remote work and an advocate for our clients and the remote work community. Anyone joining the team will be evaluated on their remote work advocacy and the proficiency of their remote work skills as defined by our professional certification criteria and established best practices because they are role models for the best practices we teach. We talk about this in our interview process, incorporate it in our new hire orientation, introduce it in our new hire training, and practice it throughout an employee's time with us.

If your mission and vision define the organization's purpose, the core values are the heart and soul of how we operate as individuals and as a team. Core values are the fundamental beliefs we live by translated into action e.g., how we behave as we work and interact with others. As Sophaya's founder, our core values reflect my personal values. As you set up your plan, identify your core values based on what matters to you, your business objectives, and what kind of team culture you want to build.

Here's an example of mine taken from Sophaya's and the RNI's handbook:

At Sophaya, we don't take ourselves too seriously, but we take our work very seriously. We like innovative ideas, trying new things, we welcome change, and we value each other for who we are – both our strengths and weaknesses. We aren't perfect, but every day we strive to be better, and we always operate with our core values in mind:

1. *Do what you say you are going to do, be honest when you can't*
2. *Have a global mindset – consider the downstream impacts*
3. *Hold yourself and each other accountable*
4. *Take responsibility for your actions – own it, learn from it, and move on*
5. *Give people the benefit of the doubt – trust but verify*
6. *Always ask the question, don't assume*
7. *Stay humble and remain open to feedback*
8. *Be curious and open to change*
9. *Say it to my face – employ the 24-hr. rule*
10. *Keep learning, get out of your comfort zones at least once a day*

11. *Treat people the way you want to be treated, always with respect*
12. *Have compassion, but set appropriate boundaries*
13. *Listen and imagine yourself in the other person's shoes*
14. *Ask for help early and give help gladly to those that need it*
15. *There is no shame in failure – learn the lesson and apply it next time*
16. *Respect difference and see the strength in diversity of thought*
17. *No one knows everything - sometimes you teach, sometimes you're taught*
18. *Practice reciprocity, show gratitude, remember to watch out for each other*
19. *Nothing is perfect, but it needs to be good enough to be proud of*
20. *Always take the high road, lend a hand to those in need*

It's up to you to define your organization's mission, vision, and core values. We have 20 core values, but I know of very successful companies that operate with less than 10. One longtime retail client of mine has just five; **dedicated, honest, fun, confident,** and **colorful**. I love that last one, don't you? Many team leaders introduce core values at the team level as well. One leader I knew, Brian, a very skilled remote executive working in financial services, always made a point of addressing everyone by their name whether they were in the room, on a call, or on a video screen. Brian had responsibility for a very large, international team of several hundred remote employees. His team worked in different countries, spoke many languages, and had different skills. Brian's simple gesture always had an enormous impact on his folks. It was a show of humanity that made them feel seen, valued, and part of a team. His people always relaxed a little, smiled more, and sat up straighter in his presence. This leadership approach aligned with Brian's primary core value: **Everyone has value and deserves respectful recognition as a person.** He role modeled it every time he interacted with anyone. It worked particularly well in Brian's international team as his values transcended culture, language, and work location.

No matter the size of your core value list, take the time to define how these values translate into behaviors so you can give clear examples to your employees when you introduce them to your remote team. Core values are subjective and open to interpretation. Remember, even dedicated, well-meaning people are messy. Without guidelines, core values like "colorful" or "fun" can be interpreted in lots of unusual ways. Providing parameters will save you and your employees a lot of headaches down the road. Guidelines and defined performance expectations provide measurability so it's easier to set employees up for success, evaluate their behavior, and provide feedback for performance accountability. Defined mission, vision, and core values are particularly important for remote teams. Don't cut corners as these elements become the foundation for team culture and influence the "virtual workspace." They provide meaning and help build team cohesion because they tie the team together. As a member of a remote team, employees can't point to an office building and say, "I work there." Remote team culture exists independent of location. It's the intangibles that draw employees in, help them feel part of something special, and give them team pride. Mission, vision, and core values are less concrete than an office building (pun intended), but when applied thoughtfully and translated into visible behaviors and concrete operational practice, they are a powerful force that helps a remote employee feel connected and valued.

Be prepared to take a lesson from my friend, Brian. Always role model your core values if you want your employees to take them seriously and adopt them as their own. Team trust depends on it. Trust is built remotely the same way it is built-in person. Actions speak louder than words and consistent action that aligns with the words spoken speaks loudest of all. You can tell a remote employee you have core values, but they will only believe your values are real if they see those core values consistently translated in your everyday behaviors. I saw this play itself out with one client, a national retail chain, where the staffing and recruiting team behaved in ways contrary to the company's stated core value: mutual respect. While the majority of the team embraced the value and it showed in their treatment of others, the company's head of HR had a hard edge to her, and she created a negative culture within her team because she consistently failed to treat people with respect. This leader consistently behaved dismissively with interviewees, new hires, and employees in distress. She showed little compassion, kindness, or regard for anyone. Conversely, the company CEO, President, and VP of Operations were highly customer focused and emotionally intelligent. They made a point of emphasizing the company's core values as their differentiators and they openly role modeled positivity, fairness, and friendliness with everyone. This disconnect caused a lot of division and underlying tension throughout the organization. Remote employees avoided the HR leader whenever possible, or they adopted her attitude. Turnover was high, and it was hard stabilizing the staff. When the labor market started to tighten and employees had better options, turnover skyrocketed and hiring stalled. Exit interviews indicated many remote employees distrusted the company's sincerity in their message of mutual respect because they perceived the head of HR was allowed to routinely violate the stated core values.

Those exit interviews were a measurable metric as were the staffing and turnover numbers indicating the company had to act. It was possible to identify a base set of behaviors related to the company's stated core values. Those behaviors were then added to job descriptions, performance appraisals, discussed in one-on-ones, and inserted into other operational goals. They became criteria for identifying top talent, promotions, and employee recognition programs. When this happened, non-conforming or inconsistent behaviors that were out of alignment with the core values were identified, addressed, and corrected quickly on an individual basis. The core values started to be more than words. People saw them as important; they took them seriously, and eventually, the core values became a shared and cherished point of pride across the organization. During this initiative, the head of HR left the organization when it became clear she had no intention of changing her behavior. Her departure accelerated a change in morale and sent a positive message to the staff that stayed.

Business Goals and Deliverables

Business goals and deliverables help define priorities and work processes in daily operations and business execution and can be tied to measurable outcomes. The best business goals for remote employees start at the company level then cascade down to the functional level to allow each remote employee to understand how their daily work tasks contribute to the company's overall performance. The more specific the goals and more they link directly to work process, business outcomes, and tangible business results; the more defendable they are as a performance measurement tool. When these goals are tied to daily tasks, it helps an individual remote employee see how they fit into the process and understand the "why" behind the work. When goals and deliverables are executed and achieved in accordance with the company's mission, vision, and core values, the results are highly engaged teams that can executive self-sufficiently. Conversely, misalignment can create dissonance and frustration in your team. Seek to integrate each of the performance metrics discussed in this chapter so they support each other and work in harmony for the best results.

I can't emphasize enough the importance of measurability. Your remote employees undergo high level scrutiny because they work outside an office and measurability gives you (and them) a fighting chance to demonstrate their business value regardless of their work location. In remote teams, different metrics serve different purposes and measure different things. Mission, vision, and core values help shape organizational culture and provide the foundation for team interaction and engagement. But they can be seen as "soft" or a less tangible measure of business performance unless they are tied to tangible behaviors that can be evaluated e.g., showing respect to others by meeting your work deadlines on time or alerting team members in advance if you are unable to meet your deadline as planned. This may seem like a small example, but it highlights many of the remote work best practices we've discussed in previous chapters – self-awareness, self-discipline, self-accountability, conscientiousness, showing respect for others, communications, respectful interpersonal interactions, through a work performance and business delivery lens.

Even though 2020 demonstrated remote professionals can do their jobs effectively, lots of entrenched skepticism remains toward remote work. Many executives, middle managers, supervisors, and team leads, used to a traditional office structure, are particularly eager to bring everyone back in the office because that's all they know. It will be a lot of work convincing these folks of the possibilities. They view remote work with suspicion as many have over-romanticized office life and they lack the remote leadership skills to make the transition to remote team leadership. Even faced with meaningful metrics, these folks will struggle if you adopt a remote work business strategy. Anticipate the mental shift many of your leaders need to undergo to see the business value in remote work. Having tangible business metrics will help you measure your plan and allow you to present hard evidence remote work is good for business.

What does a business goal look like for a remote employee? Here are just a couple of examples of performance metrics tied to business goals and deliverables rather than workplace:

■ Increase top line revenue by 15% by acquiring six new business clients by the Q2 of this calendar year.
■ Complete documentation of our new accounts receivables process and create a central virtual repository that is accessible to all A/R finance team members company-wide by March 31 of this year.
■ Reduce customer service representatives (CSRs) turnover by 7% by designing and implementing a new CSR recruiting and training process that can be delivered equally effectively in-person or remotely. Deadline for completion: December 31 of this year.

Consult your team for additional performance metrics that are meaningful for your business and align with your business goals, then add them to your plan

Universal Performance Metrics

Universal performance metrics are behaviorally based measurables applicable across all job descriptions. Like the universal competencies that I'll discuss in Chapter 7, they enable you to build a single cohesive performance review process and team collaboration standards in multi-disciplinary, remote teams. Universal performance metrics focus on interpersonal behaviors and must support the team culture you want to build. They provide a framework for evaluating your team individually and how they interact as a group. These metrics may feel vague at first, but team leaders and individual managers can drill down and define the behavioral specifics as they relate to the job role, mission, and core values. For example, communication may mean one thing for account managers with customer facing roles versus a project management role that emphasizes interdepartmental collaboration. Make your performance metrics as straightforward and specific as possible. The evaluation process for these types of metrics is based on observation of the behavior. Either you see them, you don't see them, or you don't see them consistently. This requires the evaluator to take notice of employees and how they act over time. The evaluators are managers, supervisors, team leads, co-workers, and others that interact with the employee frequently for work assignments and who can provide firsthand feedback on an employee's behavior.

Some examples include:

- Meet assigned deliverables on time according to established work quality standards.
- Treat people with professional respect at all times.
- Demonstrate a respect for difference by showing empathy, practicing active listening, and maintaining an open mind.
- Evaluate the downstream impact of your actions by seeking and providing feedback.
- Communicate effectively utilizing established communication protocols.
- Seek root cause solutions when problem solving.
- When highlighting concerns, or identifying problems, come prepared with workable solutions.
- Employ big picture critical thinking skills when executing assignments.
- Demonstrate the ability to self-organize and prioritize work tasks on your own.
- Function autonomously but proactively, keep the team informed of your progress.
- Stay open to change.
- Ask for help when you need it, offer help when it's needed.

Align your universal performance metrics with your long-term goals and cultural objectives for your remote teams as these metrics will drive individual and team behavior and impact the formation of a healthy remote team culture. Promote behaviors that strengthen the group's sense of team, build team trust, and encourage self-sufficiency. These same metrics will integrate into other areas of your talent management systems that I discuss in Chapter 7. Build a system that is consistent and aligns or your employees will feel the disconnects and trust problems will ensue.

Job Descriptions

It's hard to be accountable as an employee or credibly hold an employee accountable without a job description or, at a minimum, defined job responsibilities. In small companies or start-ups where employees must be versatile and may take on many roles throughout the workday, outlining the functional standards for each area of responsibility is more practical than trying to cram everything into individual job descriptions. As no one person is entirely responsible for a one single role and things are shifting quickly in start-ups, set performance expectations that are tied to the employee's ability to execute against many workflows or business processes rather than one defined job description. If you intend to run a lean team for an extended period, cross train your entire staff for greater team resilience and reduced business risk. Cross training keeps people sharp and makes them less resistant to change as their job role requires them to continually learn new things. By defining task responsibilities and work processes you'll be better positioned to ramp new hires up quickly as you scale and whoever is training them will have something to measure their performance against. Evaluating employee performance in this business case scenario requires observing the employee against many different functional areas and focusing on their big picture awareness, versatility, and their methods for mastering new skills. Use metrics and develop skill competencies that focus on continual learning, flexibility, adaptability, and interpersonal communication will help.

Larger companies that need more employees to handle the workload tend to hire people for a specific role. Defined roles depend on task efficiency, functional accuracy, and process or system interdependencies. Each employee has defined responsibilities and job descriptions are more straightforward e.g., finance, accounting, call centers, procurement, risk, compliance, IT, etc. Because the team is executing work that is predictable and defined, the job description will indicate the functional responsibilities, deadlines, timelines, and other relevant details. Anytime there is a prescribed daily process, a specified timeline, a reporting cycle, dependency on some calendar cycle, or alignment with other predictable, repeatable functional requirements; these types of narrowly defined job descriptions make sense. Remote teams in these roles will need additional details and training that help them understand the big picture context of the work. Each team member needs to know how their role fits into the full process and why the timelines exist. This helps employees understand the consequences of non-performance. Evaluating these types of roles is quantitative. Are deadlines met? Are results and reports accurate? Is work quality completed and delivered to established standards?

Some jobs are harder to quantify and define. Creative roles or knowledge work that are less process-oriented or system driven need a different approach to metrics as prescribed job descriptions are too restrictive and may stifle productivity and performance. Some of the other options I've discussed in this chapter such as business objectives, deliverables, universal performance metrics, and interpersonal interaction protocols are better suited as performance measures as they are less dependent on how the work gets done and allow for more flexibility in this area. But these remote employees still need context, expectations, and some defined parameters to operate effectively and they certainly need to understand interdependencies and how their work fits into the big picture.

Functional Requirements and Existing KPIs

Most of you reading this book work in existing businesses and you are modifying things to accommodate remote work or to improve productivity in your existing hybrid remote team structure. This is to say, business operations are ongoing, and you must make modifications over time as you work hard to avoid business disruption whenever possible. That's how most of us come to remote work, as drivers of adjustments, tweaks, and upgrades to existing business models. Change can come as revolution or as evolution, but most existing businesses can't afford to shut down to retool. You may be tempted to make minor; surface changes then declare remote work victory without creating the necessary operational changes needed to support your new model. Or you could discard all existing processes and systems in favor of untested, shiny new ones while the secret sauce that made your business successful gets lost. I don't recommend either of these strategies. I've seen catastrophic business failures that employed these extremes. In business, evolution is a lot more practical and less disruptive to your existing business. It takes planning to successfully transform a company's business practices as daily operations continue. As you seek to identify metrics and key performance measures for your new remote work strategy, presumably you will have lots of existing business metrics and performance measurement options. Your task is to identify the existing functional requirements and key performance indicators (KPIs) that are most relevant for measuring progress toward your desired future state regardless of where the work gets done.

You'll get the best results if you follow the process I've outlined and establish clear long-term goals then judiciously evaluate your current infrastructure, processes and systems against those goals. Repurpose when you can, then make considered, pragmatic choices about what must stay and what must go. As you build your remote work model, stay objective, and avoid keeping things because they are personal preferences and comfortable. Keep them if they work and they make sense and support your new strategy, discard them or re-tool them if they don't. In Chapter 8, I discuss the value of pilot programs as an implementation and change management strategy. Pilots allow you to test things in controlled, small group environments so you can evaluate them under real-world circumstances before you commit to a costly, disruptive organizational rollout or wholesale changes.

Interpersonal Interaction Protocols

Clients often ask me how to deal with poor interpersonal behaviors in remote teams. Proactivity and working with defined purpose alleviate a lot of problems. Learning the leadership skills to implement proactive accountability, then teaching your remote team to take personal responsibility for themselves takes care of the rest. Outline the expectations up front, then hold people accountable when they violate them. It really is that simple. In Chapter 7, I detail Sophaya's Accountability Cycle™ that provides the structural framework for the process and the steps to implement it. Employees in remote teams are still people even if they are remote. If you want them to behave in a particular way, they need to know what's expected. Then they need feedback, so they know when they are meeting expectations and when they are not. Providing consistent, balanced, timely feedback allows employees to a) continue their positive course or b) adjust and do better in the future if they aren't in compliance. Whenever you are dealing with people, things can get complicated when there is ambiguity. People's behavior gets messy, emotional, illogical, and often self-absorbed when they feel defensive, frustrated, or they are trying to avoid something. Remote team interactions can get unpleasant when this bad behavior persists, or slights are allowed to fester. In remote teams, things can break down very quickly because it's easy to avoid each other and jump to negative conclusions.

Leading remote teams is a distinct challenge because your team members work independently outside your line of sight. Assessing their capabilities and current state of mind is more nuanced and requires new leadership skills and a much more proactive, deliberate effort. Old leadership models are insufficient or downright destructive when applied to remote teams. Leading remote employees is a more collaborative partnership with leaders functioning as accountability coaches rather than a top-down power hierarchy. It requires the ability to interpret an employee's state of mind, unlock their capabilities, and enable their success using new indicators less reliant on in-person body language and physical proximity. And while the focus of this handbook is operationalizing remote work and building the necessary systems and operational structure needed to achieve top productivity; the people piece of this puzzle must stay top of mind. It's the people working within the structures you build that will ultimately determine the culture, execute the processes, and drive an organization's results.

Building infrastructure, creating work processes, and designing talent management solutions are straightforward by comparison.

At Sophaya, we focus on the people side of remote work, so I see this play out all the time. Breakdowns occur because of a lack of trust, harbored grudges, micro-management, too much hierarchy, poor treatment, overwork, or a thousand other reasons. Ironically, this is not just a remote team problem. It's a people problem. Don't assume in-person offices are any better. They aren't. Wherever there are people, there are opportunities for misunderstandings, passive aggressive behavior, poor performance, unpleasantness, and discord. However, having expectations clarified early on helps a remote team leader build a healthier team culture and establish team trust as it helps define workplace rules and an objective context for shared feedback. Feedback that is balanced builds trust and trust fosters team resilience. Healthy culture with a well-defined work structure and team trust alleviates a lot of problems because the team is more tolerant. As the team matures, it will find ways to support and moderate itself.

There is an additional layer of complexity for remote employees because they interact with each other primarily via technology. In Chapter 11, I explore the challenges of multi-channel digital communications and how and why they break down. When you design your metrics for interpersonal interaction protocols be sure to add something about the use of digital communications amongst the team. Here are just a few examples of interpersonal interaction protocols related to digital communications that can be measured by observing a remote employee's behavior toward others:

- Learn and use people's names whenever possible.
- Be extra conscious of your tone in all communication channels, when in doubt, call, or video chat.
- If you feel frustrated, stressed, or angry – pick up the phone or video chat, don't email.
- Consider the impact of your behavior on others, build trust with your remote co-workers, and check in regularly so you know what is working and what's not.
- If you are in a bad mood, it will impact how you interpret other people's intent, pause, and take a deep breath before you react.
- No one can read your mind, speak up and let others know how you feel, do this explicitly, as hinting isn't helpful.
- Don't initiate gossip or spread rumors, hold confidences, be professionally discreet.
- Once an issue is resolved between parties, let it go, move on, but continue to maintain accountability with each other.

- Give others the benefit of the doubt unless there is a clear trend, then address it privately and directly.
- If you are having a hard day or are struggling in some way, speak up and let someone know.
- Be direct but professional rather than hint or engage in passive aggressive behavior.

Remote Team Meeting Protocols

The business world is dependent on meetings of all kinds. Meeting-centric corporate cultures have always existed. Meetings certainly have their uses but when meetings are piled on top of each other, and they become the bulk of the workday, that's a problem for remote team productivity. Too many meetings kill remote team productivity and add a lot of unnecessary stress on individual team members. Your remote employees need time to get their work done and if their schedules are jammed with meetings that can't happen. Meeting fatigue isn't a new thing, we've done this to ourselves for a very long time even in in-person offices. Remote teams are prone to meeting overload because remote teams are out of sight. Managers use meetings to micromanage or keep their people visible. It's easy to underestimate the negative impacts because the impacts aren't immediately seen. Anyone who endured endless audio or video conference calls while sneaking in a little multitasking on the side knows exactly what I mean.

Screen fatigue is new with the meteoric rise in video conferencing that occurred in 2020 and 2021. It's a real thing, but it's avoidable. Judicious use of technology, smart scheduling, effective meeting management, and an understanding of your digital meeting tools will alleviate much of the stress. You can encourage healthier meeting behavior by designing healthy meeting protocols and then measuring your team's performance against them. Build the protocols, train your people, then hold them accountable. Make it a requirement for all remote team members to learn virtual meeting best practices. Add it to team goals, performance reviews, and criteria for promotion so it is a meaningful, highly visible metric. I guarantee three things will happen: a) Team productivity and morale will improve, b) Stress levels among your people will go down, and c) Your bottom line will get better. Don't believe me? Take a minute and calculate the cost of the average meeting in your company today. Use your own meeting schedule for one week. Calculate your hourly rate then multiply that by the number of hours you spent in meetings this past week. Now do it for a month. Now do it for a year. Using this calculation, I once helped a commercial banking client save tens of thousands of dollars and positively improve their team productivity simply by helping them re-tool their approach to meetings.

All this said, meetings have very practical business uses and for remote teams they play a special role. Meetings are important touch points that bring colleagues together, provide social contact, provide an opportunity for vital information sharing, and allow the team to propel work forward. When executed strategically and thoughtfully, meetings are a powerful tool for engagement. Yes, it will cost you money to train every one of your remote employees best practice virtual meeting skills, but the business return is clear and measurable. I've touched on this in just about every chapter. As a metric measure, effective meeting skills are as important as multi-channel communications, meeting your work deliverables, and acting with integrity in your interactions with your co-workers. Effective virtual meeting skills must be non-negotiable for any remote employee and remote team leader. Make it a priority to hire employees with these skills or, at minimum, a capacity to learn them. Build these skill requirements into everything you do – your new hire onboarding process, remote work job descriptions, professional development curriculums, leadership and top talent programs, and your operating protocols so people take them seriously and understand their value.

We have a lot of distinct types of meetings these days and each meeting format has unique variables. At RNI, we teach best practices that are universally applicable for any meeting structure whether it is in-person, remote, or a hybrid meeting format. These universal best practices are equally effective for small group meetings e.g., project meetings, one-on-ones, team meetings, etc. as well as large group events e.g., town halls, all-hands meetings, division meetings, etc. Because of their dependency on technology, virtual meetings are moderated forums and there are specific accommodations that help drive engagement and keep meetings on task and useful for meeting participants. For example, video platforms need extra attention before, during, and after meeting time and active moderation during the meeting. For a typical meeting between small working groups, you can get away with conscripting meeting participants to help you with some of the meeting logistics. Large meetings are a different story, I've addressed them separately at the end of this section. Here are some examples of universal remote meeting best practices to get you started.

Examples of universal remote meeting best practices:

- Define the meeting objectives up-front.
- Only invite the people directly involved with the meeting objectives.
- Prepare an agenda and send it out in advance.
- Indicate your expectations for the meeting so people know why they are invited and how to prepare.
- Start on time.
- Build in a little social time at the beginning to get people talking.

- Actively moderate and keep participants on task.
- Use techniques like "parking lots" to capture ideas that are off topic but need attention later.
- Have someone take notes.
- End early or on time.
- Follow-up with a clear recap of notable decisions and to-dos.

In remote teams, group meetings primarily take two forms, a) all virtual with everyone joining a single video or audio conference instance or b) A hybrid format with some participants attending in person and some attending remotely. Each meeting type has unique characteristics, and your meeting protocols need to take them into account to be effective. Infrastructure plays a critical role in remote meetings because of the many technical requirements. I discuss infrastructure in detail in Chapter 3. Access to systems, devices, platforms, and internet bandwidth requirements to support your chosen technology tools are critical. Any manager or employee holding virtual, or hybrid meetings must learn to verify, manage, and functionally operate those technical variables. Meeting protocols must include mastering the technical stuff, but there are also logistics, physical tasks, and best practices for moderating as well. For example, your virtual meeting protocols must address the pre-meeting planning process, the role of the moderator, and the need for some sort of production support to manage the technology during meetings of any size.

Best Practices for Effectively Executing Fully Virtual Meetings (All Participants Virtual Logging in from Their Individual Devices)

Virtual meetings are logistically easier as meeting participants will gather in the same virtual space. Because your meeting "room" is virtual, the technical considerations are a priority and need to be addressed well before the first group meeting occurs. Choose your tools, learn the functional capabilities, and test things out in advance. Trust me when I tell you, there are ALWAYS unexpected things that occur – technically and behaviorally when you are reliant on technology. It is in your best interest to discover how the virtual environment functions in advance of your meeting, so you look good on meeting day. Because meetings are an important touch point, particularly for remote and dispersed teams, I urge you to use video whenever possible. The visuals are powerful and after the initial shock of it, participants will get so used to using video that they will miss it if video cameras aren't on for some reason. Generationally, you will be forced into it eventually as Millennials and Gen Z-ers are always on camera. As younger professionals enter the workforce, they will bring this preference with them. Given how cost effective and widely available video is, there really is no excuse anymore. Just do it.

Pre-meeting planning:

■ Follow the universal meeting best practices I listed earlier.
■ Identify a meeting moderator, chat monitor, and note taker if your meeting has more than just a couple of participants. Don't try to do it all yourself.
■ Assign to-dos for each role indicated above so everyone knows in advance what they are doing on meeting day. You can have one person do more than one role e.g., one can monitor the chat and take notes if they are well versed in the technology.
■ Identify the meeting platform appropriate to the invitees.
■ Make sure all your participants have access to the platform.
■ If your meeting is video based, make sure your participants have the bandwidth, software access, and devices needed to participate e.g., cameras, microphones, internet access, etc.
■ When the meeting invitation is sent, add login or dial-in information as well as the meeting agenda.
■ Decide meeting logistics in advance e.g., will your meeting be recorded, does the meeting require a password, will participants be muted as they arrive, will you require cameras on for video, etc.
■ Inform the meeting participants what is expected in advance so they can prepare.
■ Practice with the technology prior to the meeting if you are unfamiliar with it.

Running the meeting:

■ Open the meeting platform in advance of the scheduled meeting start time to ensure connectivity if this is your first time using the platform or the first time the group is meeting.
■ Greet participants by name as they arrive.
■ Use the time when participants are gathering before the meeting kicks off for informal chat.
■ Start the meeting on time, alert the participants if you are recording.
■ Moderator must review the meeting format and requirements, e.g., cameras on, on mute when not presenting, etc.
■ Inform participants of the steps they can take to join the discussion e.g., adding requests in the chat window, raising their hands, moderator will call them by names, etc.
■ Have the chat monitor watch the chat.

- Build in quick breaks for meetings over one hour.
- Role model good virtual meeting practices throughout the meeting.
- End on time.

Post-meeting follow-up:

- Send out meeting re-cap with key decisions, meeting highlights, to-dos, and task ownership.
- Include a link to meeting video recordings (if relevant) in your recap notes.

Best Practices for Hybrid Meetings (Some Participants are Physical Present in a Meeting Space, and Others Log in Remotely)

Hybrid meetings are complex and more problematic as they combine all the logistics of an in-person meeting with all the logistics of a virtual meeting. The meeting host must technically connect the two worlds then actively moderate throughout the meeting so all participants can work together effectively. Most people underestimate how hard this is and remote participants are most impacted. It's painful to attend these types of meetings and see the in-person participants disregard, ignore, or forget their remote colleagues. Poorly run hybrid meetings create resentments, destroy team trust, and encourage team division. These meetings send the unspoken message that remote participants aren't valued, and they are lower on the team hierarchy. Don't underestimate how much damage they can do. On the flip side, a well-run hybrid meeting is refreshing and energizing as it happens so rarely. An old colleague of mine, Mike, always understood the power of these moments. Every team meeting, he showed respect to everyone on his team and required all his in-person participants to acknowledge their remote colleagues as well. Mike role-modeled this approach and made it a universal team expectation. As a result, his very large, international team-built trust, a healthy team culture, and was highly productive. Mike accomplished this by emphasizing his expectation that team members focus on how people treated each other rather than their geographic location. His team internalized this value.

Pre-meeting planning:

- Follow the universal meeting best practices listed earlier.
- Identify a meeting moderator, chat monitor, and note taker ahead of time.
- Assign to-dos for each role indicated above so everyone knows in advance what they are doing on meeting day, emphasize the need to help remote participants feel a part of the meeting.

- Identify the technology necessary to enable full participation for all attendees.
- Make sure all your remote participants have the access and devices they need.
- Choose a meeting room in advance and work through the technical logistics beforehand.
- If your meeting includes video, make sure your remote participants have the bandwidth, software access, and devices needed to participate e.g., cameras, microphones, internet access, etc.
- Make sure your meeting room is enabled with video capabilities so all participants can see each other.
- When a meeting invite is sent, add login or dial-in information and the agenda.
- Decide in advance if the meeting logistics e.g., will it be recorded, will cameras be on, does it require a password, will participants be muted as they arrive, will you require cameras on for video, etc.
- Practice with the technology prior to the meeting if you are unfamiliar with it. Test the room and the remote access to ensure everything functions as planned.

Running the meeting:

- Open the meeting room and the technical platform in advance of the meeting time to ensure connectivity on all sides.
- Greet participants by name as they arrive – in person and online.
- Use the time when participants are gathering for informal chat, encourage chat between in-person attendees and remote attendees from the start.
- Start the meeting on time, alert the participants if the meeting is being recorded.
- Have the moderator review the meeting format and requirements, e.g., meeting etiquette for all participants, in-person attention to remote participants, repeating group questions for all to hear, cameras on, on mute when not presenting, etc.
- Inform participants of the steps they can take to join the discussion and remind them of the unique logistics e.g., repeat questions for remote participants, pay attention to in room audio devices, avoid side chat, adding requests in the chat window, raising their hands, etc.
- Have the chat monitor keep a close eye on the chat window and use it to transcribe group questions or comments from people in the room.
- Build in quick breaks for meetings over one hour.

■ Follow the universal best practices throughout the meeting.
■ End on time.

Post-meeting follow-up:

■ Send out meeting re-cap with key decisions, meeting highlights, to-dos, and task ownership.

Today there are lots of cool tools for video conferencing – software, apps, devices, and specialty gadgets specifically designed to support hybrid meetings. If you are currently relying on the old tabletop audio conferencing devices, it's time to upgrade. When you upgrade your technology, upgrade your moderation skills as well. A great moderator helps all meeting participants feel welcome and works to get everyone's voice into the discussion whether they are in the room or in cyberspace. Unless you make these significant changes, you are short changing your remote team members and denying them the opportunity to contribute business value. If you have high turnover or suffer from low team engagement within your remote team, I'd assess your approach to meetings as a starting point. How you conduct meetings may seem an unlikely place to start, but meetings are so pervasive, they touch everyone in the team. It's an easy skill to train and an effective productivity measure. Prioritizing meeting protocols will give you immediate positive impacts and yield strong returns for minimal investment on your part.

Managing Larger Group Meetings

In remote teams, you will have times when large group meetings are the best, most efficient method for conveying information quickly. These are potentially powerful forums and there are lots of different ways to organize them for maximum business and team cohesion effects. Large remote or hybrid meetings are productions. Treat them as such. They require more planning up front and are best executed with a support team and a moderator with experience in these forums. You don't need a big team, a small, dedicated group will do. But it's important they fully understand the technology, have crowd engagement skills, and are well versed in the technology platforms you use. As part of the pre-meeting planning, make sure there is a back-up plan in case something goes wrong technically. If the moderator gets disconnected for some reason, a support team member needs to be able to step in at least temporarily. If the meeting host gets disconnected, the moderator must be prepared to step in as needed. Most large group meetings like this benefit when they are hosted by senior leaders or respected members of the senior staff that are trusted voices within the group.

The good support team will ensure the leader can be seen and heard by taking care of the logistics quietly in the background. A skilled moderator helps convey important logistical information to the audience and skillfully manage the crowd so the leader can focus on presenting their message effectively.

Leader-Led virtual events are a cost-effective way to support change, influence culture, and build a sense of community. These can be produced quickly and easily; they don't need to be highly polished. Anyone with a smartphone or computer can record a video message, then distribute in an email or moderate a livestream town hall with audience interaction and open Q & A. These forums are best if they happen on a predictable, routine schedule so the employees get used to the forum format and see it as a routine communication rather than something to dread or fear. It's an interesting time when the mass adoption of social media has taught us the importance of bringing our message directly to our audience. There are huge downstream benefits to the team and the business when you set up these types of meetings.

During 2020, I helped many clients set up town hall forums, all-hands meetings, strategic planning, and other one-to-many meetings that were extremely effective in getting timely information out quickly to large, dispersed groups. Senior leaders and C-suite executives can gain intimate access to everyone in the organization in real time and cost effectively deliver a message directly to an entire team. I've seen organizations like the White House do this extremely effectively. During the Obama presidency, one of his top advisors, Valerie Jarrett, held the first White House live stream virtual public form for small business owners hit by the 2008 financial crisis. Leveraging real time video and chat, she took questions real time from an extremely nervous business audience. Valerie took one of my questions right after I posted it, it felt as real as if I was in the room holding my hand up in person. Back then it was novel and compelling. Now we see it happen all the time on social media platforms with individuals holding live discussion forums. In remote organizations, events that give leaders access to large groups circumvent conventional hierarchy and eliminate the need to cascade a message down many levels, thus avoiding the inevitable message mangling that occurs when information passes from one level to the next. It's a highly effective tool and when used strategically, is a very cost-effective way to create team camaraderie, promote a healthy team culture, and positively boost team morale.

Highlights

A business and a team can't sustain themselves without accountability and performance measures that indicate progress toward established business goals that are in alignment with a company's mission and values. As individual employee contributions and behaviors together dictate business success or failure, ensuring there are clearly defined metric measures that speak to work performance, team interactions, and work requirements are necessary as they give each employee and their leader a baseline to measure against. The critical elements that provide this baseline for ongoing performance evaluation and accountability include:

Organizational mission and core values

- Mission and core values direct the way business gets done and what kind of culture you wish to develop.
- Mission and core values will dictate many of the operational decisions you make and inform how work gets done.
- In remote teams, vision and core values form a virtual office culture when your remote work operating model and business structure both support and are informed by them.
- Since remote teams are unable to acquire culture through more traditional means, no informal contact in the hallways or lunchroom, mission and core values provide remote teams with a sense of purpose when they are actively practiced.
- When considering your mission and core values take into account your remote business model and remote work operating structure.

Business goals and deliverables

- Business goals and deliverables provide a framework for accountability and performance measurement.
- Old measures such as coming to the office and physical presence are meaningless in a remote workplace, goals and deliverables transcend work location and provide a more concrete method of evaluating work performance.
- Once goals and deliverables are set, communicate them to the team and prepare to provide your employees with the tools, training, and resources appropriate for a remote work operation.

Universal performance metrics

- Universal metrics are performance measures that apply to all employees regardless of their job function, length of service, and position with your organization.
- Universal metrics are often behaviorally based and form the basis for a portion of the performance review process that is applicable to everyone.

Job descriptions

- Job descriptions in remote teams indicate who does what and defines individual team roles.
- In remote teams, they perform a necessary function as they help explain team interdependencies and work boundaries.

Functional requirements and existing KPIs

- Leaders in existing businesses moving to a remote work operating model will need to assess and evaluate existing functional requirements and KPIs as the existing structure is unlikely to lend itself to remote work.

Interpersonal interaction protocols

- Remote teams are made up of people. Misunderstandings and miscommunications are inevitable.
- Plan for this up front by defining the expectations for interpersonal interactions, communicating them to your employees, then holding people accountable.
- Role model the behaviors always as your actions will speak louder than any words you speak.

Remote team meeting protocols

- Remote work meetings require more upfront planning as they are moderated forums that depend on technology and active facilitation to achieve useful outcomes.
- All virtual meetings are simpler to plan because everyone is in one virtual place.
- Hybrid meetings are more complicated as some people are physically present and some are online. The facilitator's job is to engage everyone equally.
- Remote meeting forums allow one leader to address a large group efficiently but should be treated like a production with upfront planning and a team for support.

Chapter 7

Component Four: Talent Management Systems

Our next component focuses on the talent management and the HR structural systems that support a healthy remote employee lifecycle. These systems pertain to your biggest business expense and your most important business asset, your people. In this chapter, I'll outline how these talent systems support every aspect of the remote employee lifecycle and how they have been largely overlooked. As people make job choices based on a job's potential and how they are treated once they take the job, much of the content here directly correlates to job satisfaction and turnover. The specific elements I've included are:

- universal remote work skills and competencies
- compensation, benefits, and employee policies
- remote team recruiting and hiring
- 30–60–90 onboarding systems
- leadership accountability cycles
- performance review process
- career paths for remote employees
- disciplinary process

Universal Remote Work Skills and Competencies

There are specific, measurable business skills and competencies that lend themselves to successful remote work. You can hire them, teach them in your training programs, and incorporate them as you design career paths and promotion criteria. Utilize them along with your cultural values as you build out your talent management processes. Universal remote work competencies help you rethink your candidate profile and re-tool your recruiting process so you can hire for the right remote work talents. They formally highlight the unique skills required for remote work and allow your remote employees to be acknowledged for their remote work talents. The universal performance metrics I discussed in Chapter 5; flow from these work skills and competencies. Keep everything in alignment with your culture and business goals. That alignment provides cohesion and helps elevate awareness that remote work takes unique skills.

To show you how these pieces fit together, I've included an example of a universal remote work competency model I built for a financial services start-up looking to staff up quickly due to anticipated rapid business growth. As an early-stage start-up, they had yet to build out talent management systems because the original team was so small. They had acquired a substantial round of funding and planned to double or triple the size of the team quickly, the founders wanted to target their hiring efforts for the short term as they simultaneously built out the talent management systems. I aligned their identified competencies with their stated cultural values, then drilled down to define the supporting behavioral attributes, and finally identified the skills training needed (Figures 7.1, 7.2, 7.3). Then we used the information to craft job ads and interview questions targeting the needed skills. Finally, we designed an onboarding process and built new hire training that all aligned with the company's aggressive growth goals and supported their remote team operations structure. Here is my template, I keep it simple so I can focus on moving things forward quickly. Use it to make your own plan based on the needs of your business.

Compensation, Benefits, and Employee Policies

Compensation

Traditionally, companies benchmark employee wages against regional cost of living standards rather than job description, experience, or demonstrated capabilities. This means employees doing the same job get paid different pay rates depending on where they lived. Current data shows that workplace flexibility will play a big part in attracting talent for the foreseeable future. When labor markets get tight, employers will adopt flexible options to attract top talent, or any talent for that matter, and they will pay whatever they must for it. The advantage of a remote labor workforce is your talent pool is much larger. As an employer, if you are willing to provide remote options when others are not, you have an immediate advantage. As this becomes more common and employees start to recognize their

Remote Work (RW) Competency Model
Building RW Talent Management Systems

Company Cultural Values: Growth oriented, Collaborative, Entrepreneurial, Relationship-focused, Ethical

Critical Thinker
Personality Attributes: Proactive, independent problem-solver

Skills	Skills Training
Analyzes available data	Critical thinking
Thinks big picture	Data analysis
Evaluates solutions against business goals	Strategic thinking
Conducts root cause analysis	Root cause analysis
Seeks timely input from experts	Risk analysis
Makes intuitive evaluations	Business writing
Decisive	Leadership

Entrepreneurial
Personality Attributes: Open-minded, tenacious, self-motivated

Skills	Skills Training
Seeks problems to solve	Critical thinking
Productively questions status quo	Communication
Self-organized	Time management
Takes initiative, self-motivated	Business planning
Remains objective and outcome driven	Project management
Initiates collaborations with others	Change management
Can independently devise, but collaboratively execute a plan	Risk analysis
Can pivot and adjust to new circumstances	Leadership
Willing to take calculated risks	Strategic thinking
Adaptable to change	Tactical execution
Open-minded, flexible thinker	Critical thinking
Strategic networker	Networking skills

Figure 7.1   How to align employee competencies with company values

Collaborative

Personality Attributes: Team-minded

Skills	Skills Training
Shows respect for difference	Interpersonal communications, Emotional Intelligence
Seeks outside expertise to accelerate problem-solving	Strategic networking
Considers the impact of their actions on others	Interoperability, Emotional Intelligence
Manages stakeholders effectively	Stakeholder management
Evaluates downstream impacts and acts proactively to mitigate them	Political savvy
Supports younger team members and actively mentor them	Project management, Leadership
Celebrates team achievements	Change management, leadership
Shares credit	Teambuilding, Negotiation
Willing to share knowledge with others	Leadership, Collaboration

Inquisitive

Personality Attributes: Life-long learner

Skills	Skills Training
Shows curiosity about things, actively seeks to understand the big picture	Interpersonal communications
Actively seeks out information from credible sources	How to mentor
Continually strives to improve and grow	Innovation topics
Takes initiative to drive own growth	Leadership
Strives to improve own skills, learn and apply lessons learned	Operationalizing change
Accepting of the learning process, able to be comfortable not being the expert	Emotional intelligence

Figure 7.2   How to align employee competencies with company values (continued from Figure 7.1)

Ethical

Personality Attributes: Acts with honesty

Skills	Skills Training
Considers ethical implications of a business deal	Business ethics
Acts honestly at all times	Critical thinking
Acknowledges the contributions of others	Communication
Raises concerns professionally and productively	Legal/Risk/Compliance

Relationship-focused

Personality Attributes: Emotionally intelligent

Skills	Skills Training
Actively works to develop relationships with others	Emotional intelligence
Seeks to provide value to and show appreciation of others	Networking, Emotional intelligence
Considers others during planning and execution of work tasks	Business development, Implementation, Project Management
Is an effective networker	Diversity, equity, inclusion
Shows tolerance for views other than their own	Conflict management, Emotional intelligence
Considers other points of view with an open-mind	Managing challenging conversations
Manages disagreements and conflict professionally with a goal to preserve the relationship when possible	Leadership, Negotiation, Emotional intelligence

Figure 7.3   How to align employee competencies with company values (continued from Figure 7.1)

competitive market value, candidates will ask for market wages tied to industry standards rather than geographies. Prepare yourself for this as it's already starting to happen particularly with candidates with specialized, in-demand skills in the life sciences and other STEM (Science, Technology, Engineering, and Mathematics) fields as well as other specialized professional services.

Remote work is also a viable business strategy for retaining current employees who are highly valued. This is a particularly successful bet when the employee is established, respected, and highly skilled. Because they are already trusted, have an established performance record, and are culturally integrated, making the jump to the remote when a family circumstance demands it, is painless and relatively easy. I have lots of examples of highly skilled folks who successfully made the switch. Retaining good employees is cost effective, less disruptive for your business, and reduces the load on your team overall. If you have a top performer ready to leave because of a move or personal issues, consider thinking out of the box to save them. I know lots of notable examples of employees who made the move to remote areas without leaving their employers.

Aida worked in a large financial services company that had no work from home policy. She was a successful and highly prized project manager with a strong track record. She had the respect of her boss and her peers, and she had been identified by her company as a top performer with a bright future with the company. When she got engaged and her fiancé received an excellent job offer in another state, Aida assumed her only option was to resign. This meant giving up her seniority, potential future promotions, and leaving before she was fully vested in some of her benefit plans. Not only would the move cost her money, but she really loved her job, so after she and I talked, Aida started exploring other options. Even though her boss was skeptical, she valued Aida so much that they worked out a 6-month trial that allowed Aida to transition to a remote position with quarterly trips back to the home office for check-ins. Aida got married, made the move, and several years later she was still working remotely and was an active role model and mentor for several younger colleagues who aspired to work remotely, too.

Bill was an experienced mechanical engineer with specialized product knowledge and lots of positive client relationships. His company relied heavily on him for all sorts of complicated implementations, and he was the lead on many high-profile projects. His boss valued him personally and professionally. But Bill worked in an urban location that suffered from ever-increasing traffic problems. His commute had risen steadily over the years, and he was spending more than three hours in the car going back and forth to work. Bill was tired of the commute, tired of cold weather, and his daughter, who lived out of state, had recently given birth to Bill's first grandchild. With all this happening, he reached his limit and wanted to quit. His boss offered him an alternative. Bill could move wherever he wanted, he could eliminate his commute by working from home, and keep his job with the company. Bill took him up on the offer. He moved closer to his daughter who lived further south, transitioned to a remote lifestyle with no commute, and had a renewed commitment to his job and company because of their willingness to accommodate his quality-of-life concerns.

I'm seeing this tactic employed in less traditional industries as well. Recently, I was working with a multiple-specialty healthcare organization that was about to lose their highly proficient, very experienced clinical practice manager, Tara. Tara was well respected by everyone and had established herself as a consummate remote team leader. Well-liked and beloved by her clinical staff and the physicians, Tara kept on top of things even though she was rarely onsite because the clinics were spread out across the state. Her clinical teams were in a panic because Tara had handed in her resignation due to an unexpected move out of the area when her husband received an excellent job offer. After an extensive search, only one candidate applied for Tara's job, he was less experienced, had a spotty work history, and his requested salary was $30K higher than Tara's salary. I suggested to Tara's boss, the Medical Director, that Tara, working remotely, was a far better option than paying more money for an unknown candidate of questionable talent.

Tara already did much of her work remotely because her team was so dispersed. Plus, she had successfully worked off-site for much of 2020 and 2021 due to health concerns so there was precedence for this unusual approach. While the Medical Director and I built the business case for the plan, Tara identified several members of her team that she identified as "practice leads" and set them up to be her eyes and ears in the clinics during operating hours. By leveraging the remote work operating practices that Tara and the Medical Director had successfully implemented at the start of 2020, and training Tara's chosen practice leads, Tara went remote without incident. After just three months, the overall impact was a net positive for everyone. The organization kept a trusted employee, the clinical staff gained new skills and achieved greater resilience, the clinics continued to function efficiently without disruption, and the patients received excellent care.

These are just a few small examples of a larger trend toward leveraging remote work as a retention strategy in new, creative ways. No point in losing talented employees that you have already invested in when remote work is a viable business alternative. In all three of these cases, the employee stayed with their company, had renewed commitment, and maintained their same pay rate even though they moved to a new region. I can hear you telling me, "You don't understand, it's not possible to go remote in my industry." I'm not saying every position can go remote nor do I want you to pay more than you can afford to outspend your competition. What I am saying is these are the trends you are up against. If you want to establish yourself as an employer of choice in this new era of flexible work, start revising your thinking about what's possible before you reject this alternative. Review your compensation and benefit plans as well so you are ready when your Aida, Bill, or Tara come to you with a workable plan. I am asking you to keep an open mind and explore all your options. Examine the possibilities with a fresh set of eyes before you reject them and consider the market advantage of becoming the employer who makes innovative changes before your competition does.

Benefits

When it comes to employee benefits, think about equity. If you have a hybrid business model, whatever benefits you have for your office employees, how will you replicate them for your remote employees? Lower pay and perceived lesser benefits for remote employees send a clear message, remote employees are not valued by your organization in the same way office employees are valued. Office employees who are not allowed flexible work options will feel your remote employees have something they do not. Either way, it sets up an adversarial relationship between office employees and remote employees. If you give up your physical office space, you must find new ways to substitute desirable perks for your employees. Luckily, many of today's employees are looking for lifestyle options that still afford them a chance to advance their careers. Do your research and ask your people what they really care about, then include some of those features in your benefit plans. Check legal requirements in your state of incorporation and be aware that as you bring on remote employees, you are subject to their home state laws as well.

Employee Policies

As the workplace shifts and new remote work operational models emerge, you will need to update employee policies, so they comply with the current legislative requirements and align with the rest of your remote work plan. Best practice for any organization is to design your workplace policies so they are based on job requirements rather than work location to avoid discriminatory practices and use the accountability cycle I discuss in this chapter to avoid creating one standard for office employees and another for remote employees. Use common sense and avoid punitive remote work policies that assume guilt up front. It's better to rely on the accountability cycle I've laid out for you that relies on operational structures and performance accountability based on defined, job-related expectations. By following the formula I've outlined for you, your policy manual will focus on universal criteria and specific performance expectations. Then you can invest in training for your managers and staff to help them build the necessary skills needed to work consistently both individually and as a team in this new, self-accountable way.

A lack of skilled talent in local markets will force many organizations to re-examine their recruiting efforts, staffing and retention plans as well as compensation models, benefit options, and the supporting employee policies. Compensation, benefits, and employee policies for remote employees are going to be an ongoing discussion for the foreseeable future. Currently, workplace transformations are far ahead of legislation. Partner with smart remote work experts who are keeping track of the shifts in the legal landscape. You don't want to get caught by surprise. For the latest information on all these topics, including remote work best practices, market trends, links to current expert discussions, and the latest remote work legislation, visit our website, the Remote Nation Institute, at www.remotenationworks.org and sign-up for our monthly remote work newsletter.

Remote Team Recruiting and Hiring

First impressions are important, in remote teams, even more so. When business leaders ask me the best ways to engage their remote teams, I always tell them that a cumulative, "drip" approach is best. Remote employees will absorb your company culture based on how they are treated day-to-day rather than how you describe your culture in a welcome video or your employee handbook. Videos and handbooks are important, but they can work against you if they paint a rosy picture that contradicts their personal interactions with their boss and other team members. Remote employees pick up on disconnects quicker than in-person employees. Be careful to assess every stage of your recruiting, interviewing, onboarding, and new hire training process. Make sure they align and support your cultural goals. Even more importantly, observe the behaviors of the employees responsible for the process delivery as their attitude toward and treatment of the new employee will have more of an effect than the process itself.

I once worked with a large retail client with a very dispersed, national team. The company leaders were great people, working hard to build a lively, friendly team culture. They describe themselves as dedicated, honest, and service driven. The company's compassionate, caring senior team really invested in its people and worked hard to treat people with respect. Most of the line managers and supervisors lived and breathed the values and were exemplary leaders and role models. However, over the years the organization struggled with high turnover in certain key positions. Some of it was the nature of the work, but the company invested a great deal of time, effort, and resources to help new remote team members feel welcome, supported, and included. That certainly helped convince some employees of the company's genuine interest in its people. Yet upon close assessment, I discovered there were several individuals who had a lot of contact with new employees in these high turnover groups that failed to live up to the company's cultural standards. They were poor cultural role models and consistently presented an unfriendly, surly demeanor toward new team members. Some of the recruiters and new hire trainers were downright mean. These new employees got mixed messages as many people they worked with embodied the cultural promises and treated them with kindness and respect, but these exceptions did not. This created continual, high turnover in areas with the most exposure to these poor cultural role models as the employees with the most contact with the mean folks found it hard to trust the company's stated cultural message was sincere.

The lesson is clear, whatever cultural values you define as important will only have meaning if you and your team demonstrate those values in your actions and treatment of others day-to-day. In remote teams, every person is a role model for someone and anyone working with new employees or young team members must be made aware of the impression they create as representatives of your company, and it's stated values. As you develop your remote work business model, invest in choosing employees that exemplify the characteristics you define as important. Emphasize the need for everyone to be conscious of the impact of their actions on others. Make it a part of every talent management and performance accountability system you build. Pay special attention to your recruiting and hiring practices and the people implementing them. Every point of contact, from your job postings to the way job candidates are treated, interviewed, onboarded to your team, and managed daily creates the culture in your team. These cultural touch points will have a direct impact on team engagement and will directly influence employee turnover. I've seen it time after time. The reality of daily treatment starting with the first point of contact and the consistency of the follow-through day after day will make the most difference in remote employee engagement and team morale long term.

A quick note, some of you outsource your recruiting and staffing functions to third-party vendors. Pick good partners that you are proud to have represent your organization with everyone applying for a remote job with your company. Applying for a remote job and participating in a remote interview process are part of a new remote employee's first impression. Make sure it's a good one by negotiating the process you want followed as part of your recruiting contract. When your new remote employees get the best treatment possible, it provides a positive start that makes it easier to engage them from day one. That positive impression is never wasted. A dear friend of mine always says, "Even if we are unable to hire them or they choose not to join us, they are potential customers or word of mouth referrers and they deserve our respect."

30–60–90 Onboarding Systems

I'm going to tackle the elements of a new hire curriculum and performance evaluation process in this chapter when I discuss workforce training. However, the reason I included it here is to emphasize the opportunities that exist to communicate culture, build positive team collaboration habits, and cultivate engagement at the very moment when an employee is *most* excited and open to influence – the moment they accept the job, transfer to a new team, or are promoted to a new position within your team. Newly hired, transfers, or promoted remote employees that have a positive, team-oriented experience during their first 30–60–90 days on the job come away with a higher degree of team trust and a deeper sense of commitment to their role and responsibilities. Having a structured new hire, transfer, and promotion training process is the first step, but you can really make yours stand out by adding a personal touch. Choose respected role models from within your team to help you build, implement, and administer your new employee process so everyone on the existing team takes part and benefits from their participation. Then elevate the impact by showing your newbies the love.

Take a lesson from the hospitality and customer service industries. Apply a personal approach to this tender time in the employee's life cycle and use the first 90 days to make new remote employees feel special, supported, and at home. Just as the hospitality industry and highly renown service-oriented companies like Zappos and Warby Parker pay attention to the tiny details to make an experience special, so can you. Send new employees a welcome gift with company swag to put something tangible into their hands branded with your company logo. Not only is it a kind gesture, but it links the new remote employee to your company and labels them part of the tribe. At Sophaya, we send every new team member a branded "Club Kit" with fun Remote Nation gifts, stickers, and a handwritten welcome card to show them they are now part of something special. Have fun with it.

Design traditions that help your newbies visibly interact with the rest of the team. Introduce them by name at video team meetings, assign them team mentors, and acknowledge early wins. Build in strategic touchpoints to do pulse checks and gauge the remote employee's state of mind. How are they feeling about their decision to work with you? What do they need? What's working and what's not working for them? Include plenty of opportunities for the new remote employee to interact with the existing team individually and as a group so everyone can get to know each other. Build team interaction into the first 90 days so the new employee can begin to form relationships and develop trust. For newly promoted team members, set them up with mentors and advisers who have gone through a promotion, so they have resources to help them navigate the politics and added responsibilities of their new jobs. These advisers can help reduce stress and provide a confidential sounding board, giving the promoted employee a trusted confidant to turn to when they need to work through sensitive situations.

Finally, leave plenty of time in a 30–60–90 schedule to set expectations and get the new remote employee used to receiving lots of feedback. Receiving a lot of feedback will likely be a big adjustment as most employees receive little to no feedback during their professional careers. They may associate feedback with getting in trouble and it makes them nervous. Remote employees that are left on their own and who don't get regular feedback, get disengaged, and feel underappreciated fast. You need to get them accustomed to LOTS of feedback early on as it normalizes the feedback process and gives people a sense of where they stand. You want all your remote employees to view feedback as something that's to be expected, valued, and actively sought.

The Leader-Led Accountability Cycle

We sometimes delude ourselves into thinking that making employees show up to a central office on time is equal to holding them accountable. It isn't. Having a traditional office structure and physical proximity to your employees isn't a guarantee of employee productivity, good work performance, or behavioral compliance. Capability and excellent work performance are not tied to physical presence. Just because you can see someone sitting near you doesn't guarantee they are productive, effective, or engaged. The reality is it's hard to evaluate any employee's work performance – remote or in person – if there isn't some agreed upon standard to measure against. If you don't have work performance criteria defined and you haven't learned the leadership skills to follow-up on them effectively, you can't hold any of your employees accountable in meaningful ways.

Throughout the previous chapters, I've emphasized the importance of definition as that definition is so foundational to performance accountability. No one gets up in the morning, looks in the mirror and says, "I'd like to fail today." But without clear operating guidelines, that's how many people feel at work. They view success as a moving target, and remote employees get discouraged, stressed, and frustrated when the workplace is ill-defined. When a team is remote, this lack of clarity will make it impossible to build trust and team cohesion. If you want to achieve remarkable things with your remote team, your employees need to learn the rules and requirements of their job. Then they need to feel those rules and requirements are applied fairly and objectively. To achieve true, fair performance measurement you need a systematic approach to performance accountability that lends itself to the realities of a remote team structure.

Once you have expectations and standards defined and you've communicated them to your employees, then accountability really begins. Healthy performance accountability has three distinct attributes; a) defined structure, b) meaningful sharing of feedback based on observation of performance against that structure, and c) frequency, consistency, and objectivity that builds trust. That's why I've built all of these attributes into my Leader-Led Accountability

How Do You Measure Remote Work Performance?

Use the Sophaya™ Leader-Led Accountability Cycle

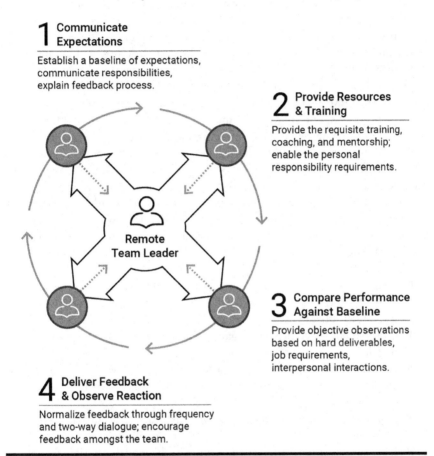

1 Communicate Expectations

Establish a baseline of expectations, communicate responsibilities, explain feedback process.

2 Provide Resources & Training

Provide the requisite training, coaching, and mentorship; enable the personal responsibility requirements.

Remote Team Leader

3 Compare Performance Against Baseline

Provide objective observations based on hard deliverables, job requirements, interpersonal interactions.

4 Deliver Feedback & Observe Reaction

Normalize feedback through frequency and two-way dialogue; encourage feedback amongst the team.

Figure 7.4   The Sophaya™ Leader-Led Accountability Cycle

Cycle outlined in Figure 7.4. Leader-Led Accountability is a four-step process that enables remote team leaders to evaluate work performance and build positive team productivity in remote teams. The steps are deceptively simple:

Step #1 = Set expectations.
Step #2 = Observe performance.

Step #3 = Provide objective, timely, and balanced feedback.

Step #4 = Observe the impact of the feedback and start the cycle again by reiterating your expectations once again.

In practice, this is an entirely new way of leading a team that shifts the focus away from a traditional command and control approach to proactive coaching, mentoring, and collaboration. It requires something different from the leader and the employee – maturity, personal responsibility, and autonomous self-discipline.

If it feels like I am shifting a bit and getting a little more nitty, gritty tactical in the next few sections, I am. These components are important to a remote employee's success, and they are distinctly different from traditional leadership models. I'm providing you a little more operational detail and specific tactical insights to inspire you to take a hard look at your current company practices. The Leader-Led accountability cycle is a departure from traditional leadership models as it shifts the roles of both the remote leader and the remote employee so each must take responsibility as an equal partner in the work. The leader sets the context for work performance so there is clarity as to what an employee is accountable for, and the employee is accountable for performance delivery.

In this model, leaders:

- Define roles and responsibilities effectively communicated to the team.
- Provide the training, support, and resources necessary for the employee to learn their job and execute it.
- Observe employee behavior against the stated expectations and defined metrics.
- Provide objective, timely feedback on their observations to alert the employee of their progress, success, and to redirect when performance falls short.
- Normalize feedback through two-way discourse so feedback flows both ways.
- Deliver a consistent, diligent application of the model over time for a positive cumulative effect.

Employees also play a part. They are expected to:

- Meet work performance expectations.
- Behave in accordance with the stated values.
- Contribute positively to the team culture.
- Hold themselves and each other accountable.
- Act in accordance with the stated values and cultural norms.

There is no substitute for defined performance metrics, explicitly communicated expectations, and a leadership accountability framework that consistently alerts remote employees of their achievements and missteps against a defined, articulated standard. The goal is to hold employees accountable and provide ongoing feedback that conveys concrete acknowledgment of a job well done and redirection with coaching, training, and needed support when it's not. In remote teams, this is essential because each team member must perform autonomously in their own workspace; their behavior is self-directed, and self-motivated. Without routine, objective feedback, there is no way for a remote employee to judge their progress or appreciate the impact their work has on others. This feedback delivered by a manager or supervisor helps connect an employee to the work process, elevates their awareness of their impact on others, and indicates how well they are doing. When the feedback happens consistently and equitably across the team and it is balanced and includes acknowledgment of progress as well as highlighting areas for growth, it normalizes feedback and builds trust as everyone knows where they stand.

Universal standards applied predictably in alignment with stated expectations and the other elements I've discussed – mission, values, business goals, protocols, and process – create a sense of team. Combined, they are what binds the team together and helps the group develop resiliency and tolerance for change. This cycle works best when everyone has the requisite skills, will, and confidence to apply it consistently day-to-day. Leadership in this model relies on coaching, mentoring, and teaching rather than command and control or micromanagement. It also requires mature, self-directed employees that take ownership of their responsibilities, both individually and as a team. As the cycle requires all parties to assume personal responsibility for their actions, it creates a healthy virtual office culture that is positive and it enables work productivity, encourages individual growth, fosters engagement, and elevates morale. Consistent application of the Leader-Led accountability cycle takes away ambiguity and, when applied with consistency and discipline, reduces workplace stress. Conversely, a poorly executed accountability cycle that is inconsistently applied, avoids hard conversations, disproportionately focuses on catching people's mistakes, or condones poor behavior for some will create chaos

Work performance accountability is important, understanding the drivers behind productivity and operational issues is equally imperative. Use the Leader-Led accountability cycle to identify big picture operational concerns driving poor performance. The cycle requires leaders to look beyond the obvious and engage in root cause problem solving to identify and resolve the fundamental cause of performance problems. If you are troubleshooting consistent operational breakdowns, productivity concerns, or high team turnover, don't automatically blame remote employee performance. I'm not saying remote employees are above suspicion but consider the bigger picture as well. Examine the why's carefully to identify the source of your business breakdowns, e.g., evaluate the interplay between infrastructure, operational protocols, and the employees. You may well find them working against each other e.g., security procedures so locked down that completing simple business tasks is almost impossible; a lack of interoperability between your business systems and other user systems that cause work delays, poor new hire practices that fail to prepare new hires to execute on their assigned job function, or your people are dependent on tools and software that they can't access or that aren't a good fit for the business purpose.

Consult with the remote employees on your team responsible for job execution in the areas of concern and examine problems as a group. Look for trends in performance that indicate points of breakdown and work together to implement solutions that resolve barriers to superior performance. By involving your people closest to the action, leaders lighten their own load while coaching their team how to troubleshoot, solution, and resolve things as a collaborative team. As you observe performance and provide feedback, build in time to listen. Feedback works best when it is a two-way open exchange. It's a great way to role model empathy and it will tell you a lot about your remote employee's state of mind. Finally, as you are working the cycle, take good notes throughout the year and you will find year end performance reviews practically write themselves. Provide feedback on an ongoing basis. Then there are no surprises, and you give your remote employee time to recover and demonstrate their ability to master tasks and grow. It builds self-confidence, an important attribute for any remote employee, and more confident employees are more comfortable working independently. Normalizing feedback helps reduce defensiveness. It's easier to discuss a concern when your employee believes you are giving them the feedback because you want them to succeed versus if they think you're out to get them.

Performance Review Process

Performance reviews are such a loaded topic as most people have such a low opinion of them. Generally, they are executed poorly and contain feedback that is neither helpful nor accurate. Companies have long struggled with them because logic dictates there must be some framework to dole out bonuses, raises, and promotions. Yet the reality is performance reviews are often painful for everyone, and cause a great deal of bad feelings, doing more harm than good. By leveraging the Leader-Led accountability cycle I introduced in the previous section, you can change this pattern. Tie a year's worth of observing performance and feedback together into a meaningful summary that sets the stage for more ambitious goal setting for the future. It's really not that hard. All it takes is a little discipline and notetaking throughout the year.

If you use an online employee portal for your performance review process, find out if you can access it throughout the year so you can add quick notes on an employee's work efforts. If possible, make the tool accessible to the employee, too, so they can keep their own records along the way. You will be amazed at the amount of work your people have completed when you open the file at review time. You don't have to make it overly complicated, with my small staff, I make quick notes to myself and add it to each employee's file. I ask my team members to do the same. The key here is diligence, to collect a true comprehensive record. Performance reviews that are a true summary of an employee's work are energizing and a dynamic, well-rounded picture of an employee's work life. Tying performance review to the accountability cycle helps you to support an employee's growth and link your compensation and bonus structure to real achievement and business contribution. The performance review closes out last year's work effort, summarizes progress made, and then it's time to start the cycle again by setting new, more ambitious goals that address the business needs and the employee's current capabilities, ambitions, and growth interests.

Career Paths for Remote Employees

Often remote employees are left out of career opportunities or passed over for promotion because they aren't top of mind, or the company has no system for keeping track of top talent outside of their home office. Traditionally, if a remote employee was lucky enough or politically savvy enough to advance their career outside their work region, they relocated to a new region to take on the new role. If they were unwilling or unable to accommodate a relocation, they turned down the opportunity. This is such a waste of existing resources that are already on a company's balance sheet. In many instances today, relocation isn't necessary. Employees know this. As many employees reconsider their willingness to move for a job and they seek flexible work options that can accommodate them, companies that add flexible, remote career paths for their remote employees will be an instantly attractive alternative. Internal candidates know the company, understand your business, and have a proven history of performance. Well-trained, skilled remote employees are even more valuable as they have the attributes that are the foundation of good remote team leadership. They are prepared to lead a flexible workforce. But you can't benefit from this talent if you don't know it exists.

In smaller organizations, keeping track of talent is easier particularly if you make it a priority and build it into your talent management systems at every step. The Leader-Led accountability cycle supports this as it relies on continual performance evaluation that becomes a more useful performance review.

Everything I've discussed up to this point provides the raw data you need to create a meaningful talent database. This doesn't have to be complicated to start, even the smallest remote team can keep records manually, then build it into their strategic plan to watch internal talent for career advancement. Larger organizations have lots of options, too. There are so many ways to electronically track skills and talent today. Look for employee portals that align with Leader-Led accountability and track an employee's accomplishments. Can your current employee portal be leveraged as a searchable talent database with a little tweaking? If you do not have an employee portal but are considering one, think about it as more than just a static, electronic file cabinet with name, date-of-hire (DOH), and a performance review tool. Check out functionality and see how far you can leverage the tool to help you support the accountability cycle, performance reviews, and tracking internal talent. Create your own internal LinkedIn talent database that gives you insights into the talent residing within your company now.

Just as employees are openly expressing interest in flexible work options, there is a noticeable shift in an employee's willingness to "wait their turn" for career growth. Younger employees are vocal and impatient, this is putting pressure on companies to reconsider how they define career paths when they wish to keep their current employees engaged. I see this in my own staff as I bring in new talent and as I work with interns. There is a steady shift away from the idea that a worker will graduate, join a company, and stay with that company for their entire career. Some of this is coming from our over-glorification of the cult of entrepreneurism and our fascination with the select few under-30s who achieved enormous wealth through their start-ups. Some of it is coming from the proliferation of shows that promote the search for undiscovered new talent in entertainment, fashion, and cooking for a quick trip to fame and fortune. But for the rest of us mere mortals, many people entering the workforce today have seen family members experience a layoff, job transition, or bad labor markets or they have had these experiences themselves. Some companies accept turnover as inevitable and use it to maintain lower wages or to right a balance sheet particularly in publicly traded companies worried about their quarterly earnings reports and the short-term impact on their stock price. All this combined with other social factors have permanently changed employer – employee relations.

This works in an employer's favor when there is an excess of workers as employees stay around out of fear and necessity. However, when the labor market tightens and employees are scarce, companies must get resourceful to attract, engage, and retain talent. Remote work programs that widen your talent pool, provide the flexibility that employees seek, provide clear growth opportunities, and help your people see an interesting pathway forward for themselves at your company give you an edge. I experienced this myself many years ago as an operations manager working in a labor market with an unemployment rate of under 1%. When faced with this reality, I got highly creative extremely fast. By retooling our approach and building systems that invested in my existing team while also retooling my entire talent management process. By thinking creatively, we were able to accommodate the candidates that were available to us as well as reaching beyond our traditional candidate profile and hiring geography. Over time, by focusing on engagement with the existing staff, we were able to become an employer of choice. Then word of mouth from our existing staff gave us a lift as our staff was so enthusiastic about the work environment that they told their friends.

Disciplinary Process

I'm getting very tactical in this section because holding employees accountable is difficult for many leaders. A lot of people avoid dealing with anything that feels like conflict. It's not unusual for unskilled or less experienced managers to turn a blind eye and let things pass. In remote teams, this lack of follow-through leads to no good. Allowing non-performers or poorly behaved team members to linger or act with impunity erodes your professional credibility and negatively impacts team trust and morale. If a remote employee appears to be a non-performer, but the cause of the problem is lack of system access, poorly explained expectations, incomplete training, or some preventable issue and the employee starts to fall behind, you and other team members can jump to the conclusion the employee is slacking when really, they weren't set up for success. If you fail to do your routine check-ins and follow the accountability cycle because you assume the employee's performance is willfully negligent, everyone will suffer needlessly.

In remote teams, things can get bad fast as failing employees react defensively. I've seen many cases when avoidance or passive aggressive behavior in a remote team causes team members to lose trust and isolate themselves. Because they are out of your line of sight, they can disengage and if they are really upset or feeling resentful, they can do real damage if they are so inclined. You can avoid a lot of headaches by taking a more proactive approach. Do regular pulse checks to learn your people and gauge their state of mind. If you sense something is off, address it immediately with open ended questions and compassion. "You don't seem like yourself today, I'm worried about you. Is everything ok?" Then use active listening and pay attention to what they say or don't say in response.

Remote employees are people, and everyone has a difficult day once in a while. Assume the best in your people until evidence proves otherwise. Tackle things as soon as you notice them, before they grow into something big. When handled with humanity and compassion, these conversations present a real opportunity for skilled remote leaders to strengthen trust boundaries and redirect someone who is struggling. If the source of the problem is something simple e.g., someone isn't feeling well or a remote employee is having a tough time at home, you have an opportunity to show you care and strengthen the relationship through swift and empathic action. Great remote team leaders are proactive when managing poor performance and inappropriate behavior. They see these moments as a chance to uphold their values and test their accountability skills. When these incidents go smoothly, they provide the team with positive role models for managing conflict amongst themselves. I realize dealing with emotions can be stressful and uncomfortable. However, it's unavoidable at times. People are messy. Even the most skilled performer will have difficulties occasionally and need your support. We all will misstep sometimes and make mistakes. Accept that no one is perfect – not even you.

It's a leader's job to give everyone under their charge the best chance for success. However, not everyone will be good at everything and not everyone can succeed as a remote employee. Sometimes this early intervention will cause you to question an employee's capability to meet the requirement of their job. This doesn't mean they are bad people, but it may mean they aren't the right person for a particular role or maybe they aren't suited for remote work. As you adjust your candidate profile, interviewing process, and launch your 30–60–90-day new hire training you give yourself a better chance to identify candidates well suited for the role, your organization, and the remote work lifestyle. But even then, some people won't make it. Prepare yourself for this in advance by following the accountability cycle from the first day of employment. Then listen to your new hire trainers and have a process in place so you are ready when it happens. You can give everyone you hire the best chance of success and avoid many misunderstandings and daily pitfalls by building a solid remote work operating plan, setting clear expectations, and taking time to develop effective work systems that support remote work at every stage of an employee's time with you. Even then, people will sometimes fail to meet performance requirements or act inappropriately. It's up to you to initiate corrective action quickly and professionally.

Because remote work is so segmented, it can be difficult to stay on top of everyone, particularly early on in your remote leader tenure. It may feel like something pops up spontaneously without warning. But there are always signs if you keep your eyes open and really focus during your routine check-ins. Learn your people and do those routine pulse checks. This may feel like a lot of work initially, but it's a necessary part of the job. Think of everything you learn about your employees as data that when closely examined, will give you real time indicators that all is well, or problems are brewing. When your team is remote, always evaluate the situation in the big picture context. Do what you can to identify the underlying drivers fueling the behavior. Ask lots of questions before you jump into action. What do you know about the employee? Is this typical behavior? Has it happened before? What is this employee's work record to-date? Has anything changed recently? If this is your first time working with remote teams, I urge you to develop your skills in this area as quickly as possible.

Use the normal feedback process to check-in with the remote employee. Ask if everything is ok. Use video so you can see their body language and facial expressions. Listen carefully as you may discover the cause of the behavior isn't a disciplinary problem at all, instead, something is happening at home, there is confusion about an assignment, or there is an operational issue that needs fixing. If that's the case, respond accordingly. If you discover the employee does need a behavioral redirect, address it quickly and directly. No hinting or innuendo. It's important you are explicit, objective, and straightforward. You can do this professionally and respectfully, but the information you deliver needs to be clear and unambiguous. When you provide continual feedback and that feedback is balanced, then occasional redirection is a normal part of the process. Remote employees appreciate it because it gives them a clear sense of where they stand. Nine times out of 10, a simple private conversation will resolve the issue. Never use email or other text-only digital communication channels to inform a remote employee there are concerns as they may misinterpret and miss your point. Address issues of concern via video, phone, or if practical, in-person. The rule is praise in public, but redirect, reprimand, or deliver a disciplinary message in private.

If things continue after your first redirect, determine the appropriate course of action by following your established disciplinary process to reprimand, suspend, or terminate them. In remote teams this process will happen at a distance. Use video for visibility and ask a second person to participate to take notes and witness the proceedings. Provide the remote employee with a specific recovery plan with clearly defined consequences so the employee has their best chance of recovery. Deliver the plan via video, phone, or in-person. Never, ever use email, text, or instant messaging (IM) for this delicate purpose. I do recommend you use email to send the re-cap of the meeting containing the details of the plan to the remote employee as this re-cap will now become an official documented record of what's to come next. Your re-cap must include plan details, who is responsible for what, timelines, and the specific consequences for non-compliance. If you haven't done so already, get other key members of the team involved e.g., local leaders who know the employee and may have physical proximity to them and other key resources such as HR. In Chapter 11, I'll discuss multi-channel communications in more detail, so you fully understand the risks of using the wrong channel.

Follow-up on the plan is critical. Stay on top of things, follow your normal accountability cycle process, and provide the appropriate plan support. If you observe the remote employee making progress, acknowledge the effort. If there is no progress, or worse, performance dips even further, don't wait to act. Keep a close eye on the situation and do the necessary preparation in advance if you see things moving in a negative direction. Remote employee terminations have special logistical considerations e.g., system access removed, email re-directed, equipment returned, termination paperwork filed, etc. If you do have to terminate a remote employee, debrief after the event, retain the lessons, and apply them for continued improvement.

Highlights

The third attribute of any remote team is its people. Remote employees have long been undervalued by their employers and employers have paid a price for this in lower workforce productivity, higher turnover because of low remote employee engagement, and a failure to fully realize full ROI (Return on Investment) of the talents of their remote workforce. To gain the maximum business value from remote employees, talent management processes that provide meaningful career opportunities, recognize talent, and promote equity and parity for all employees regardless of work location are a necessity. The most important components of a healthy remote work talent management system include:

Universal remote work skills and competencies

- Successful remote employees possess a distinct set of business skills and capabilities than office workers.
- Traditional competency models designed for in-person employees are not applicable for remote professionals.
- Companies adopting remote work as a business strategy need to identify the requisite remote work skills that best support their circumstances and align their competency models accordingly.

Compensation, benefits, and employee policies

- As you adopt a remote work operating model, it is necessary to review your compensation, benefits, and employee policies so they support your new remote work structure.
- Paying remote employees less shows disrespect and indicates a lack of understanding of their value.
- Show your remote employees the same respect you show your in-person employees and compensate them based on contribution and delivered value rather than workplace location.

Remote team recruiting and hiring

- The remote employee recruiting and hiring process is the first point of contact you have with a new remote employee.
- Design the recruiting and hiring process so it helps set expectations and positively introduces the new employee to your company mission, core values, and company culture.
- Adopt a hospitality approach to your process and build a positive, engaging experience with a wow factor.

30–60–90 onboarding systems

- New hire training is a mini-version of the Leader-Led accountability cycle.
- Prepare the process in advance and hand pick your new hire trainers as your brand ambassadors.
- Tailor each 30-day cycle so it contains functional training, cultural training, team integration activities, and lots of two-way feedback so everyone knows where they stand.
- Work to fully integrate the new remote employee into the team, but objectively evaluate them to ensure they have what it takes to do the job.
- Seek to position the new hire for independence and self-directed autonomy by the end of 90 days.
- Assign team mentors and go-support to address questions past the first 90-days and fully integrate the new hire into your Leader- Led accountability systems going forward.

The Leader-Led accountability cycle

- Leader-Led accountability is a four-step process that enables remote team leaders to objectively evaluate work performance and build positive team productivity in remote teams.
- Step #1 = Set expectations.
- Step #2 = Observe performance.
- Step #3 = Provide objective, timely, and balanced feedback.
- Step #4 = Observe the impact of the feedback and start the cycle again.
- This is an entirely new way of leading a team that shifts the focus away from a traditional command and control approach to proactive coaching, mentoring, and collaboration.
- It requires something different from the leader and the employee – maturity, personal responsibility, and autonomous self-discipline.

Performance review process

- In this new model, a performance review is a comprehensive summary of an employee's performance over time.
- For a new hire, this means a performance review every 30 days for the first 90 days of employment.
- For an existing employee, the length of the cycle is determined by the organization.
- A typical cycle lasts 12 months.
- It's important for leaders and employees to keep a journal of performance so the review is a true reflection of the feedback – good or bad – delivered over the full period.
- After the performance review, the accountability cycle resets with more ambitious goals that reflect the progress the employee achieved during the previous year.

Career paths for remote employees

- Traditionally, organizations have failed to recognize the business value of remote professionals.
- Companies rarely build meaningful career paths for ambitious and skilled remote employees, to incent them to stay long term.
- This is an area of opportunity and is a necessary addition to any company's talent management cycle if they choose to adopt a remote work operating model.

Disciplinary process

- Discipline is a natural part of the accountability cycle.
- If an employee fails to meet expectations, it's your responsibility to let the employee know your concerns asap.
- Address concerns just like you address all feedback, with open ended questions seeking data that will help you discern the root cause, then apply the appropriate solution.
- Give employees the benefit of the doubt but set consequences for further non-compliance.
- Give every employee the best chance to succeed.
- Accept not everyone will – be prepared to take quick, but professional action when necessary.

Chapter 8

Component Five: Remote Workforce Training

In remote teams, ongoing professional development and specialized remote work skill training are not an academic exercise. They are an important business imperative and a strategic tool for building a healthy remote team culture and a skilled, confident team. As with many of the things I've discussed in this handbook, there are many ancillary benefits when training is executed with conscious alignment. Investment in continual professional development is an operational necessity as remote employees are most successful, resilient, and open to change when continual learning is a team value that gets measured and is baked into the accountability cycle and the performance review process. That is why I encouraged you to add life-long learner as an attribute to your candidate profile and competency model in Chapter 6. Integrate professional development and skill training strategically into your remote work operating plan as an engagement tool and a mechanism to keep your remote employees positively honing their skills.

Skill training is a way to activate your remote employees and build team camaraderie when you schedule real time, livestream interactions that provide shared group experiences. Program curriculums that include internal and external participants from different disciplines or experienced team members with real world functional expertise promote better team collaboration, help foster relationships, and highlight team capabilities. When everyone goes through shared programs, that community experience creates powerful alumni networks that you can leverage to form mentoring programs, support groups, and other

DOI: 10.4324/9781003243557-8

dynamic engagement mechanisms. Align training with your professional development plans for individual team members and use everything to build team productivity, encourage collaboration, and foster team trust. There are many benefits when you build a dynamic learning culture that promotes self-confidence and rewards remote employees for remaining curious and open to change. As with some of the other sections, I'll discuss tactics as well as strategic considerations, specifically I'll cover the need to:

- **integrate new hires thoughtfully**
- **upskill leadership**
- **rethink mentoring**
- **build team resilience**
- **incorporate contractors into your culture**
- **encourage continual learning**

Integrate New Hires Thoughtfully

As soon as you select a remote candidate, make them an offer, and they accept a position on your team, the clock is ticking. Once they sign that offer letter, you have a short window to create a memorable, positive first impression by delivering a unique and welcoming new hire experience. To a new remote employee joining your team, training is how they will learn their job. But remote employee new hire training is so much more than that. As a remote team leader, recognize that new hire training teaches functional expectations, workplace protocols, essential work skills, team tool functionality and conventions, as well as team culture, the norms for interpersonal interactions, and the team's personality. Forming positive relationships with team members at this early stage helps engender trust and will have an impact on whether the new employee is comfortable asking for help when they have questions.

As all employees go through new hire training, the new hire training program can provide a universal language among your remote team, a shared common experience that binds them, and, when done well, can convey a tangible indicator that the remote team members are part of something special. In Chapter 7, we discussed the 30–60–90-day approach as a tool to connect your new remote employee to the company and the team and I laid out the strategic considerations of the new hire training process. Tactically, the 30–60–90-day format (Figure 8.1) addresses the learning needs while acclimating the new remote team member to the Leader-Led accountability cycle. The goal of this training is to prepare the remote employee for self-sustaining independence while also positively binding them to their colleagues and the ins and outs of your remote team

Charm Your Remote New Hires

Build an onboarding system that includes functional knowledge and adopt a hospitality approach that supports positive engagement and cultural integration.

Day 1
Starts with interview & offer

30 Goal Setting for First 30 Days

60 30-Day Evaluation & New Goal Setting

90 60-Day Evaluation & New Goal Setting

• Team welcoming protocols in place

• Build functional training in advance

• Emphasize feedback and peer interaction

• Advanced functional training

• More independent assignments

• Cultural mentoring, one-on-ones, shadowing

• Emphasize feedback and peer interaction

• Independent assignments, training agenda is more self-driven

• Trainer provides observational feedback on work completed

• Continued mentoring, supervisor one-on-ones, broaden peer-to-peer interactions, add committee/work group assignments

Figure 8.1 The 30-60-90 day tool connects your new remote employee to the company and the team

operating model. By chunking the training into 30-day segments, you can construct a mini accountability cycle that tracks with your growing expectations of a new employee at each stage. Set expectations and goals commiserate with each 30-day cycle. Each cycle is a building block for the next stage, work with your existing team to plan out the training well in advance. Get your best people involved – choose remote employees with great functional knowledge who are also good trainers. Since your team is remote, work location won't matter. Teach your trainers the skills and give them the tools they need to train both in person and online.

Each 30-day cycle models the accountability cycle – start with expectations, performance observations, feedback, and wrap up with a performance evaluation related to the goals set for that 30-day period. This acclimates the new remote employee to the amount of feedback they can expect once they complete their first 90 days. At the end of each 30-day cycle, provide a summary of performance, then start the cycle again for the next 30 days. Add functional requirements, team engagement opportunities, and cultural elements to each segment and make sure to add routine pulse checks so you can gauge the employee's state of mind. While you are working hard to teach them the job, connect them to your company and integrate them into the team culture. The new remote employee will need a lot of help initially to get them prepared for independence. Build in a gradual move toward self-autonomy as the new employee enters the 60-day cycle and ramp up the independent assignments during the final cycle. All this attention and close contact with a new remote employee helps you to get to know them and provides insights into capabilities, attitude, and energy. Red flags will pop up fast. Pay attention to those indicators, teach your trainers the skills they need to follow the accountability cycle steps so they can provide direct and balanced feedback. Listen to your trainers' concerns, work with them to give the new remote employee the best chance for success. Your trainers will tell you if someone isn't pulling their weight, take that seriously and terminate non-performers early to maintain team standards and to build team morale. New hires that aren't meeting expectations during the first 90 days are not going to magically get better after they complete new hire training. Non-performance at this stage is typically a sign you've made a bad hire and swift action will save you time, money, and aggravation in the long run. This said, hold your trainers accountable and evaluate their performance as well. If you are losing too many new hires within the first 90-days, assess your process and problem-solve the root cause. Ask questions that lead you to the point of failure:

- Is our hiring profile appropriate?
- Is our recruiting process supporting our culture, values, and company goals?
- Is our offer process affirming and positive?
- Are we welcoming a new hire and creating a positive experience?
- Are my new hire trainers skilled, capable?
- Are they good role models?
- Are they able to executive all aspects of the accountability cycle effectively?

Upskill Leadership

None of the plans we've covered in this handbook will work if your existing managers aren't onboard or don't have the requisite skills to support your new remote work operating model. Employees with executive leadership, management, or supervisory responsibilities at any level of your company must shift their approach to this more consultative, coaching model. Skills to run these kinds of teams are quite different, they are a huge shift for some on your existing team. Plan a heavy investment in professional development training for managers, supervisors and team leads as poor management skills will seriously hamper remote team productivity and drive remote employee turnover. Remove them from supervisory roles if they can't or won't make the change. I realize this sounds harsh, but it is a necessity. Micromanagement or command and control management approaches are annoying and ineffective in an office setting. In remote teams, they translate as distrust and suspicion and set up an adversarial dynamic that completely undermines remote employees. Skilled remote professionals don't enjoy being treated like criminals and they will only tolerate this behavior for so long. You can't engage authentically with someone you don't trust or whom you think doesn't trust you. It will be impossible for you to retain your best people, achieve remote team productivity, and build meaningful team engagement if your managers continue using outdated modes of leading. Don't blame the failure on remote work – look to the root cause. Bad management practices will cause your new remote work operating plan to fail.

Leadership and managerial competency models that align with the unique aspects of remote leadership are important as they help you emphasize your expectations of the acceptable leadership skills needed. Use these competency models guide your learning and development efforts so you can focus your efforts on building the relevant skills. Fundamental remote leadership skills include (in no particular order):

- Emotional intelligence, particularly self-awareness and empathy for others at a distance
- Multi-channel communications that align with your team communication protocols
- Leading as a coach, mentor, consultant over distance
- Multi-channel active listening
- Root cause problem solving
- Solution implementation in remote teams
- Building distance trust over distance
- Providing effective, objective, balanced feedback

- Accountability, holding yourself and others accountable with the accountability cycle
- Self-directed time management
- Managing remote stakeholders
- Managing change in remote teams
- Goal setting in remote teams
- Building engagement in remote teams
- Maintaining visibility in remote teams
- Advocating on behalf of yourself and your remote team

Rethink Mentoring

Almost every day, I listen to people tell me that remote work is bad for younger employees because it robs them of valuable exposure to experienced colleagues who magically pass on their wisdom through the osmosis of being in the office. Ok, perhaps that's a slight exaggeration, but it's not much of one. I'm told versions of this repeatedly every time I meet with a new client or present to a traditional business audience. When I ask these skeptics for specific examples of the formal processes used to foster young talent, I'm told that it happens organically and spontaneously. In many senior leaders' minds, it is a by-product of an in-person office environment populated with generous senior leaders. These interactions are apparently driven by an accomplished professional's desire to pass on their knowledge and teach younger office workers the ropes. One person told me young professionals are doomed without this exposure. We're over-romanticizing again. While I'm sure there are exceptional circumstances when experienced office dwellers extend themselves on behalf of young talent, that's not been my personal experience nor the experience of anyone I've polled over the years. This isn't a traditional corporate value, particularly in public companies. Especially ones with competitive business cultures. The reality is often quite different and rather depressing. Companies rarely have formal mechanisms for this type of information exchange. If they have something, they don't have mechanisms in place to measure its effectiveness and, sadly, teaching young professionals the "old" way often transfers bad habits and does more harm than good.

In my experience, young people are rarely noticed unless someone takes a shine to them. That usually means the younger person has the right look, background, or pedigree to be of some perceived use to the senior person. Most of the time, younger staff are relegated to the side, given lowly tasks, and told to "put in their time and wait their turn." They aren't invited to useful meetings and, many times, they are left to figure things out on their own then chastised when the result doesn't meet expectations. Interns get treated the worst, I've seen them routinely get assigned busy work tasks like filing and shredding documents for days and weeks on end. That may have been accepted in the good old days or in tight labor markets where employers called the shots. It's not the case now. This new generation of workers isn't interested in following this old model. They have different expectations and different interests. If a company doesn't meet those interests, provide meaningful experiences, and give them a voice in the process, they go start a company of their own or move on quickly to another job without looking back.

Don't assume a young person craves office life as attitudes are shifting. Yes, a young professional wants opportunities and mentoring but they also want flexibility. I warn you, younger employees are not the only ones asking for flexible options, so are women, and even older workers seeking a better quality of life. There is a unique opportunity in remote work operating models to provide that flexibility AND expose all our new colleagues – young and old alike – to interesting new business interactions because of the formats we use to connect as remote teams. In a traditional office setting, it's awkward, inappropriate, inefficient, and disruptive to have a new employee or young professional join an important in-person meeting just to give them "exposure." Imagine taking a junior team member or a new hire with you every time you get on a plane to speak with an important client, negotiate a big deal, or have old-style in-the-room face time with a senior executive. I've rarely seen it done. And I know we all want to believe we are diligent with debriefs after something momentous occurs, that we use these moments to help our teams learn the lessons and pass them on to our least experienced team members, but I rarely see much of that either.

Yet with the transition to virtual meetings, particularly video meetings, I can take my least experienced team members with me in a cost efficient, non-intrusive way. In my company, we use this tactic to accomplish multiple things at once. If we are hosting the meeting, it gives us added technical support as we assign the new employee a small role. This exposes the new remote team member to our business and teaches them virtual meeting facilitation skills at the same time. By the time a new team member completes their 30–60–90 new hire training, it's conceivable they have attended dozens of our most important meetings. This is true for our interns, too. It's a low-risk way of including team members from day one. We actively role model our remote work practices by setting expectations before the meeting takes place, providing the new employee a low-risk chance to practice with the technology in a live setting, and de-briefing afterwards to answer questions. I make a point of asking them their observations first, so I can evaluate their powers of observation and get to know how they see things. I've introduced this technique with many of our clients with great results. I recommend you add it to your 30–60–90-day new hire training process.

I've seen many organizations use virtual debrief sessions to drive team engagement and build team cohesion. It's nice when senior leaders get involved with sharing information and wisdom, but it's also powerful when peers can share with peers. Several sales organizations I know use virtual forums to conduct post-deal reviews, so everyone learns from everyone, and team members get comfortable with each other. As these are livestream video forums, anyone can attend. Younger team members are included, sometimes they are the presenters sharing their experiences. The forum moderator always leaves time for open questions. I've seen this technique used with positive effect in a product development company, engineering firm, commercial real estate, healthcare, financial service, banking, consumer insurance company, renewable energy company, etc. – the list is endless and it's growing all the time. In one healthcare organization's Grand Rounds, the forum used to review and discuss patient cases for everyone's edification, moved from an in-person meeting to an online video meeting and attendance instantly tripled. In addition, the virtual forum is now recorded so the organization is building an educational content library available to others in the future. Now the organization is considering transforming Grand Rounds to a hybrid forum with livestream broadcasts to accommodate in-person and online participation.

In addition to the examples I've mentioned, I'm helping many of my clients build virtual mentoring programs that are easier and more time efficient for both the mentor and the mentee. Because the program is virtual, there is an opportunity for mentors and mentees to connect based on interests and goals rather than physical proximity. Meetings are via video, allowing all participants to gain familiarity with video conferencing. While they participate in these programs, they are learning how to connect, build distance relationships, and network online, skills that are especially important for effective remote teamwork. This isn't just happening in companies, young people are doing it, too. I've participated in youth mentoring programs of all kinds for many years. In 2020, these programs went virtual. Now the teams I mentor have members from all over the world learning how to work together online. In case you are wondering about the value of the experience, one of my teams liked working with me so much that they hunted me down on LinkedIn after the program they attended ended. These young women lived on the west coast, I lived on the east coast, but they asked me to continue working with them to help them compete in a business competition they entered through their high school.

Their project required them to recruit a client, design a consumer product for them, then build a marketing campaign to sell the product they designed. Because of my network, I was able to connect them with some friends of mine who work for Nike. My mentees had the opportunity to learn about product design and bringing new consumer products to market from people who had real world knowledge of the process. I set my mentees up for success by coaching them beforehand and by preparing my contacts, so they understood their role as well. I had my mentees organize and conduct the meetings themselves. Then we reconvened and debriefed after the fact to discuss what they learned. As a result, they successfully helped their "client" bring a product to market. They received an award for their competition project, and they added several high-powered professional contacts to their business network in the process. My mentees were juniors in high school at the time and while their "client" was local to them and they did meet in person a couple of times, most of the project was conducted entirely online.

Build Team Resilience

Remote employees operate with a fair amount of autonomy and that makes a lot of leaders and employees nervous because they must trust their people to do their jobs. It took a pandemic to debunk the myth that remote employees were unproductive, yet many leaders are still fighting it. If you want to succeed as a remote leader, you need to continue to let this myth go. Give people the benefit of the doubt. Remote employees can be trusted if you build the virtual framework I've outlined and then skillfully apply the accountability cycle. Giving your people the benefit of the doubt doesn't mean you ignore them or leave them entirely to themselves. Don't be naïve, even office workers will get into trouble if that's your approach. Offer trust but verify performance and manage accountability for everyone, including yourself. Treat people like adults, help them build the confidence to operate to their full potential by providing them with the virtual office structure to do so.

In many ways, remote work is a mental game. You must apply self-discipline and willfully care about the impact you have on other people who exist with you in a virtual workspace. Besides remote work skills, remote employees need a certain level of self-confidence and self-awareness to do this. It requires self-sufficiency, adaptability, and a high degree of emotional intelligence. Learning to be comfortable with ambiguity and the initial discomfort of new situations helps build resilience in remote employees. All this may come naturally to some of your employees, for some it takes extra training, mentoring, and coaching to flex that mental muscle. Remote teams that internalize these qualities have a great deal of mental resilience as they are used to working with a lot of variables. There are specific tactics you can use to grow these skills in your team. I've many of the more obvious ones already, new hire training, lots of balanced feedback, role modeling behaviors, building trust, fostering engagement, etc. Others that I use regularly include special projects and stretch assignments and full cycle project work. Every one of these tactics can be delivered as part of the performance review at the start of a new performance review/accountability cycle.

Special projects and stretch assignments are work assignments outside the typical scope of a remote employee's daily job. Once you have fully integrated the accountability cycle and your employees are fully engaged, keeping them learning and interested means challenging them in some meaningful way. Work assignments that require a talented remote employee to move out of their comfort zone to learn a new skill, work with a new team, or utilize their talents in a new way help them grow and enhance their contribution to the company. I once worked for a financial service company that used stretch assignments as part of their succession planning strategy. Taking on special projects or stretch assignments in a new area was considered a typical career path that provided the employee with a big picture perspective and built their confidence. The senior leadership team evaluated these employees on their adaptability and capabilities to adapt and execute in these new work environments. As this was a company value that was measured and tangibly tied to career advancement, employees took note, saw these assignments as a positive, and actively requested them.

It's easy for remote employees to lose sight of the impact their work has on others or for them to fully grasp the operational complexities that drive work disruptions, particularly in existing companies that are moving to a remote work operating model for the first time. Learning how to successfully implement novel solutions in existing systems is a wonderful way to expose your most talented remote employees to big picture systems thinking. Full cycle project management is the process of analyzing the operations, identifying areas for improvement, applying root cause problem solving, designing a fix that is financially feasible and operationally possible, building the solution, implementing the solution, then operationalizing it. These projects can start small as process improvement assignments and they work best when there is a defined mandate and someone with experience to mentor, guide, and coach throughout the process. All the skills required to complete a full project cycle align perfectly with high level remote work and, when mastered, prepare your remote employee for future remote team leadership roles. Many of the projects I've discussed in this handbook lend themselves to this type of professional development activity – re-tooling an existing new hire process, a communication protocol, creating an integrated suite of tools to enable remote work, etc. Once your remote work operating model is up and institutionalized, use this process to address business inefficiencies.

Incorporate Contractors into Your Culture

A quick word about contractors and gig workers. They are a part of the staffing landscape in most businesses today. You pay for them, they represent you. Choose contract partners, third party vendors, contractors, and gig workers versed in remote work. Treat them with respect, and invest time in teaching, then holding them accountable to your remote work practices. In our firm, we make a point of learning our client's ways, and adopting their work tools. Yes, it's a little more work on our end, but it helps expose us to a lot of things and it keeps me and my team sharp. I mentioned this in relation to technical infrastructure vendor partners in Chapter 4. Apply the same principles to all your contract workers so they can complement rather than disrupt your remote team operating processes.

Institutionalize Continual Learning

The pace of change today is accelerating. Maintaining your remote team's edge requires forward, consistent evolution. Change is the only constant – the moment you and your people stop learning is the moment you start losing relevance and falling behind. Lifelong learning needs to be a cultural value baked into your company's DNA. Make it a job requirement that is valued and sought after by adding it into your measurement and accountability processes. Bake it into everything you do and invest in it at all levels of your organization.

Highlights

Integrate new hires thoughtfully

- You have a small window to make a positive first impression – make it a good one.
- Adopt a hospitality approach to the new hire experience.
- Construct a 30–60–90 new hire training process that mirrors the accountability cycle.
- Select new hire trainers that are great role models and excellent teachers.
- Train your trainers and provide the resources they need to succeed.
- Evaluate new hires closely, provide lots of feedback, and give them every chance to succeed.
- Terminate non-performers before the end of their 90-day cycle.

Upskill leadership

- Leaders must adapt their skills for remote teams to achieve top productivity.
- Old-style management practices like micromanagement and command and control approaches will drive turnover.

- Invest in professional development for your management team at all levels.
- Replace those that can't or won't make the shift.

Rethink mentoring

- Avoid over-romanticizing the in-office mentoring experience, it wasn't as effective as you remember.
- Don't assume young people only value in person mentoring.
- Virtual and hybrid approaches provide new ways for new hires and young professionals to participate and learn on the job.
- Virtual job-related learning forums often attract a larger audience than in-person events.

Build team resilience

- Remote employees need self-discipline, self-confidence, and remote work skills to succeed.
- Change is a constant in remote teams, learning to adapt to change is part of a remote employee's life.
- Learning to be comfortable with ambiguity and the initial discomfort of new situations helps build resilience in remote employees.
- Team resilience allows remote employees to better manage their day-to-day.

Incorporate contractors into your culture

- You pay for their services, and they represent you.
- Elevate your expectations and require them to learn your business.
- Teach them what they need to know so they can represent you well.

Institutionalize continual learning

- Continual learning is an imperative for business resilience and competitiveness.
- Adopt it as a value.
- Integrate it into your remote work operating model at all levels so your people see it as an important part of their job.

Chapter 9

Operationalizing Your Remote Work Business Model

Until now, I've focused on defining remote work, provided a business case for it, and outlined the individual components of a remote work operating model: a) infrastructure, b) operational protocols, c) performance accountability, d) talent management systems, and e) remote workforce training. Now I'm switching the focus to day-to-day operations and the implementation process. Operationalizing any business model is hard, messy, and complicated. It's also deeply satisfying. I know because it's what I've done for over 20 years. Remote work implementations are slightly different. While they touch every part of your organization as will any operational model, remote workers operate in a virtual workspace and every person on the team must learn to operate autonomously yet stay in sync with their remote team members. As I mentioned in Chapter 2, prepare to recruit a multi-disciplinary team to help. If you are a start-up, building things from the ground up, you have a distinct advantage as anyone you bring into your company will see your company's remote work operating model as the norm. You won't need to persuade them to change their behaviors if you hire well. Create a candidate profile that aligns with remote work and hire accordingly. Your remote work model may well attract them to your company. For those of you who are transforming existing businesses, it will be more of a challenge, but no worries. I've included lots of tactical information applicable to your situation as well. I recommend existing business leaders pay special attention to this chapter, Chapters 2 and 10, managing change, as the biggest barrier to successfully re-tooling existing businesses is managing people's natural aversion to change.

DOI: 10.4324/9781003243557-9

All three of these chapters deal with change concerns and the realities you will face. I've provided lots of change tactics throughout to help you along the way.

Developing a strategy and building a theoretical business model is a necessary exercise and it's an important part of the change process. Plan first, then do. Don't wait until you have a perfect plan before you get started as things change a lot during implementation but be sure to establish clear end goals as you need a baseline to measure against. It is risky to make wholesale changes to your existing business without at least a rudimentary sense of what you want to build. You need that end goal to determine all the practical stuff like resource needs, budget, and timelines. But strategy and models that are too detailed or scripted can bog you down. Don't get too attached to them. Things tend to shift so much during implementation that it makes no sense to get too invested in minute plan details.

Plans are just that, a roadmap. Just like budgets and forecasts, something that looks good on paper is meaningless if you can't make them work operationally or they aren't a true reflection of what's happening in the real world. Even the best plans sometimes encounter unexpected hurdles, and you need to be ready to pivot and even change course entirely if necessary. I was once part of a major change project that involved the adoption of a highly technical operating system that was experimental, and extremely expensive. The executive leadership team decided they wanted it then they decided planning was going to slow the whole project down, so they decided not to do any planning or testing at all. They did no due diligence before starting the implementation. Very early on, during routine testing, it became clear that the system had major operating flaws and adopting it was a serious business mistake. Since we still had time to change course, I spoke with the company CEO to alert him to the problem. I recommended we halt the implementation and reassess. But the plan was his brainchild, and he was wedded to it. Unable to accept any data that contradicted his assumed end scenario, he ordered us to continue the implementation. It was an unmitigated, costly disaster that destroyed the company. Shortly after the implementation, the CEO was ousted, the company was acquired, and the ill-conceived implementation was scrapped.

It takes a special set of skills to complete a healthy implementation process and drive critical mass adoption of any new system. Even a healthy implementation will have its bumps and you will need to tweak things to optimize them for profitability and productivity. In this chapter, I've outlined some of the field proven methods I use to take a remote work model from concept to operationalization to optimization. I explain how to:

- leverage pilots to test your plan
- build a network of remote work experts

- recruit engaged executive sponsors
- collect and analyze data to measure progress
- create a robust reporting process
- expand the rollout past the pilot

Leverage Pilots to Test Your Plan

It's always helpful to do a test run before you jump into a full system-wide implementation. A wonderful way to validate a new operating model on a manageable scale is to run a pilot. Software, app, and product developers call this process beta testing. I use this method to observe new business models in action under controlled conditions. Operational pilots give you a chance to roll out your new model with a handpicked group of early adopters, analyze it, test your assumptions, and assess the results before you do a full-scale rollout. Strategically, pilots allow you to select and train an implementation team and recruit change champions to support the full system rollout. These people can learn their role and practice working together with a lot less stress during the pilot. The limited scope of the pilot makes it easier to stay on top of things and respond to things quickly. This saves existing businesses a lot of headaches as it allows you time to identify technical system integration problems, unexpected downstream impacts, or problematic workflow issues while avoiding major business disruptions. You get to observe people's reaction to the change and use the pilot results to gain organizational support by demonstrating your ability to manage the implementation process and show its integrity. Integrating new technical elements into your existing infrastructure, building new systems, or retooling workflows to support remote work is unpredictable and tricky in an existing organization. As I discussed in Chapter 2, you need to build a multi-disciplinary implementation team and recruit a group of change advocates and change champions to work with you on your pilot. You need the necessary people involved early to address issues quickly and efficiently as they arise. Don't shortcut this step, use the pilot to gain as much support and positive momentum as possible.

Pilots are the first step in building a winning implementation strategy. They allow you to adopt a phased approach over a definable timeline. By starting small and ramping up as you build your coalition and train your implementation team, you reduce risk and allow different parts of your business to prepare in advance for the change. You will find early adopters who participate willingly in your pilot project, and a successful pilot gives you a demonstrated track record before you begin your work with more resistant groups. Pilots help you define budget and resource requirements for a full system implementation as you have real data for forecasting and project planning. Since the pilot group is small, you get to test more affordably with less operational disruption while you and the team gain valuable experience along the way. Everyone involved gains skills and knowledge in the process. Apply the learnings to improve the next phase of the rollout to gain momentum and get smarter along the way. Your team will become remote work experts that you can leverage for subsequent phases. Their participation accelerates adoption as they become vocal converts, giving you an unbiased coalition to support the change going forward as it spreads out to new areas of the company. The experience shifts people's thinking because they learn skills, gain exposure to new things, experience the process, and feel pride when things are up and running smoothly because of their hard work.

Build a Network of Remote Work Experts

You can't accomplish this implementation alone. You need a network of internal early adopters you can convert as well as a network of experienced professionals familiar with remote work business models who can provide targeted expertise and guidance. When you start your search inside your company, look beyond your typical go-to choices for candidates that will see this project as a growth opportunity. The people I know who are good at this type of work are high energy problem solvers who are undaunted by new circumstances. In your old model they may have struggled because they were always pushing boundaries. Many early adopters are curious about new things and are comfortable shifting from the typical status quo. They like to build stuff, are fast thinkers, can adjust to whatever is thrown at them and are able to iterate and adapt quickly. They like to solve problems, and don't get overly invested in plan details because they know things shift a lot during go-live. Routine bores them so after things are up and running, they will look for new project assignments. Be prepared to provide them with challenges post implementation so you can keep them as they are invaluable resources for any sort of implementation and process improvement activities. When you bring them onto your remote work implementation team, give them the plan, listen to their feedback, and once they are ready, teach them what they need to know, then manage them collaboratively using the accountability cycle I discussed earlier as they will not respond well to micromanagement.

While it's likely you will have existing employees with many of the necessary capabilities and qualities I just outlined, I recommend you seek to supplement the team with experienced remote work implementers as they can help you avoid costly missteps at the beginning when your skeptics outweigh your supporters. Plus, it strengthens your business case when you have reputable experts to calm concerns. That's what I do for my clients. I work quietly behind the scenes with the internal implementation team to provide support, coaching, mentoring, and practical advice on implementation strategy. Look for people like me who are experts in areas such as operations, change management, legal, finance, HR, IT who stay abreast of the latest trends in their disciplines. Remote work logistics are evolving so quickly, both technically, operationally, and legislatively, that it's impossible for any one individual to keep on top of every change. Choose experts who know their stuff and are willing to work alongside your team throughout your implementation, teaching them remote work skills so your in-house talent increases as a result.

Recruit Engaged Executive Sponsors

Many senior leaders unfamiliar with remote work and its effectiveness tend to be skeptical at first. Remote work challenges traditional formal hierarchy and eliminates many of the visible indicators of executive success – big corner offices, special dining rooms, executive boardrooms, and special parking places. These may sound like trivial things if your company is adopting remote work to advance itself. But you can't underestimate how much people hate giving up things they have come to believe are theirs by right. It's hard to give those things up once you have them as you believe you have earned them and are entitled to them. Remote work operating models will completely change existing paradigms as leading a remote organization is much more collaborative, less grounded in physical constructs like corner offices and parking spaces. The trappings of success are much less tangible. That makes a lot of executives extremely nervous. Because of this, building a compelling role for executives and key senior stakeholders so they can see how they fit into the future model is crucial for a successful adoption strategy. This said, there will be some that see this shift as a window of opportunity. Look for those executives who like a challenge but who have the emotional intelligence to work collaboratively.

In larger corporations, I often addressed this issue by forming steering committees that included as many influential C-suite decision makers as I could recruit. I supported the executive steering committee by providing lots of corporate communication, publicizing their involvement as much as possible and giving them a lot of visible, public credit when things went right. This may seem gratuitous, but this high-level support is critical. The steering committee put all the decision makers in the room so I could keep them informed and when I needed their support, they were up to speed, and I could keep things moving quickly. It helped me surface objections and make the necessary changes to maintain their support. This provided a firm foundation for gaining buy-in from less senior leaders in the organization as they had no desire to appear out of step with their superiors.

Steering committees provide a lot of leverage as they lend credibility to the effort, they control the purse strings, and, if steering committee members perceive some value to themselves, they become powerful spokespeople internally and externally. I worked at one large company where we adopted a new, innovative remote team collaboration technology that was very early-stage. The technology company saw our implementation as good PR for their product, as there was no conflict of interest. I was able to convince select members of my steering committee to speak on panels at industry events discussing the company's adoption of this new tool. It made those committee members, some of whom were early skeptics, look like convincing experts and gave them appealing publicity for their project sponsorship. It also earned our company positive visibility in the market as an early adopter of the new tool which in turn garnered positive media attention that increased the committee's status and the company's market profile. As a result, my steering committee members stayed engaged in the project, took a lot of ownership, and felt invested in the project's success as they, as well as the company, experienced the benefits of being perceived as cutting-edge innovators.

Executives bring a lot to the table as they can advocate at senior levels; they have access to meetings and resources that others do not. C-suite executives set strategic direction for the organization, interact with the Board of Directors, and they supply the organizational clout needed to overcome objections from their direct reports. If executives are on board, they can grease the skids and accelerate things. If they are opposed, they can obstruct and possibly derail your work. Regardless, you need as much support as possible. In addition to executive steering committees, you need working groups consisting of mid-rank leaders in charge of key areas like finance, IT, business systems, business operations, and HR to help with implementation logistics. It's much easier to gain their buy-in if the senior executive leading their area is visibly active in and supportive of the effort. In smaller companies, I seek out key senior decision-makers to gain their consent for the same purpose.

No matter the form it takes, recruiting executive sponsors from the highest levels of your organization will take time. There is an old saying, "No one ever got in trouble for saying no." Thus, executives tend to say NO far faster and much more often than they say yes. Particularly in public companies. Choose your sponsors carefully and craft the business case showing them the advantages the opportunity provides them both politically and professionally. Think about ancillary factors that can support your business case. Don't rely solely on logic or your perceived business rationale. Understand the executive's mindset, their political perspective, and what they have to lose if they support your plan, and something goes wrong. Then build your case based on all those factors combined. As with your change champions, choose well-respected individuals that other people tend to follow as well as those with considerable institutional influence. If you build a steering committee, working groups, or an implementation team that lacks institutional integrity, you are setting yourself up for an uphill battle that will quite likely fail.

Collect and Analyze Data to Measure Progress

Data comes in lots of forms. For the purposes of this handbook, I define data as information, statistics, and anecdotal indicators – some qualitative, some quantitative, some narrative – that give insights into a team's state of mind, the health of a business, the effectiveness of a tactic, the current state of adoption, impact on the business operations, and progress toward your stated goal. Data is a way of objectifying and stripping the emotion out of the situation when dealing with people so you can examine things dispassionately and strategically. It's also a pragmatic method for presenting a compelling support narrative that humanizes your implementation, grabs people's attention, and creates a sense of excitement and forward momentum. Derek Sivers talks about this in his excellent TED talk: How to Start a Movement.[1] If you haven't seen this brilliant visual demonstration of human contagion, please take the time to watch it. Gaining adoption for your new operating model is rarely so blatantly visible, so you will need to cultivate clever ways to use lots of different kinds of data to build positive attention for your plan.

Momentum doesn't happen by accident; it takes planning and conscious effort to fuel forward progress by demonstrating momentum through a combination of stats and stories. I'll get into more details in Chapter 11 when I discuss multi-channel communications. I've emphasized the need to create operational baselines to measure success and track progress to gain support for your implementation and to show progress. A thorough review of your key metrics helps you articulate your story. Revenue, expenses, employee pulse surveys, employee turnover or retention, customer satisfaction, speed to delivery, operational processes metrics, market share, product reviews, quality measures, the list is endless. Select the areas that have the most meaning for your stakeholders. Pull your implementation team together and compile a list of key points that will help you support your end goals and convey your project narrative as clearly and as simply as possible to your skeptics as well as your supporters.

Positive momentum breeds urgency, urgency drives participation, and participation activates reluctant stakeholders or non-participants (even if they aren't yet fully converted, they may give in to peer pressure). Data can't just be dry numbers. You do need hard metrics that indicate impacts on your company's profitability and operating costs so you can evaluate the hard business effects of the changes you implement. You also need interesting, fun, unusual facts as well. In Chapter 10, I'll discuss the need to expand your thinking to include data that helps you shape your change narrative in interesting ways. Data strengthens your ability to craft a compelling narrative that grabs people's attention. It has practical purposes as well. During an implementation, it allows you to stay on top of the implementation process and move quickly to fix problems or redirect your plan if something unexpected occurs. A well-run implementation helps reduce team anxiety. There is no better way to mitigate the naysayers and dissenting voices within your organization than to manage a smooth rollout. Data enables all the above.

Create a Robust Reporting Process

Not all data is actionable, operationally useful, or necessary. To fully leverage it in support of your work, it must be organized, sorted, and presented in some useful way. The goal of a business report is to transform raw data into a usable, actionable business tool that supports business decision making, both strategic and tactical, or provide operational comparisons to measure progress and proactively troubleshoot problem areas. Well-crafted implementation reports keep your project top of mind, allow you to show forward progress against your baseline and project objectives, support your communication narrative, and give you an opportunity to celebrate successes by strategically acknowledging supporters and early adopters. Reports tell the unfolding story of your implementation over time. When reports are consistent, and objective, they add operational credibility and realistically measure the impacts of the change.

Different people will respond to different data. As you design reports, do so with your end goal and the report's audience in mind. Every organization has metrics that resonate and add legitimacy to a project. For an existing business, you need a progress report that highlights key performance indicators (KPIs) against historic data so you can track the impacts of your implementation against your business performance prior to your remote work implementation. Use caution, there are limits to historic data. Your new remote work model is different from your old model so not all data is equivalent. Make sure you are selecting data equivalents from the old to the new to evaluate and compare. For new businesses, you need reports that indicate your KPIs against your projections and start-up forecasts.

All businesses will need basic implementation reports that indicate the progress and success of the implementation against the original implementation plan. Set all implementation activities to timelines and milestones with defined deliverables to ensure accountability to deadlines, key opportunities to readjust the plan or celebrate progress. These reports provide formal status update opportunities for senior stakeholder engagement and help you thank them for their support by acknowledging the impact of their participation. The key point here is business relevance and operational applicability. Develop reports that serve a true business purpose, avoid report overload. Not all data is created equal and too many reports just confuse everyone and wastes valuable time and resources. Make sure your reports have integrity and provide a balanced perspective. If a report indicates something is wrong, investigate and develop your mitigation plan so you can proactively address the questions your stakeholders are sure to ask you.

Expand the Rollout Past the Pilot

Take advantage of your pilots and plan additional phases of your rollout well in advance of the end of the pilot. As you engage in the activities discussed in this chapter, recruit your targets for phase two, three, four, and so on as you go along. Plan the subsequent implementation phases so they align with your organization's business cycle and sensible logistics. Review the calendar with an eye toward seasonal trends and cyclical workloads in each area of the company. Plan your phases when they will have the least operational disruption. If you are utilizing a steering committee, use them as champions for the implementation plan as they have the political clout needed to make it an operational priority.

If the pilot goes well and you message the project effectively, people within your organization will take notice. As you convey the results of the pilot to key members of your organization, it's not unusual for the next phase candidate to present themselves without you having to ask. You can help this process by cultivating key targets for future phases early on then entice them by including them in your critical project updates, so they feel part of things even if they aren't actively involved. That way they aren't surprised if you approach them about participating in future phases. This saves you time because you don't have to spend a lot of time giving them background as they are already up to speed on the project. When someone comes to you and volunteers to participate, appreciate this as a positive sign that you are making toward significant progress. Let this momentum carry you forward but stay diligent.

Set up good support plans to ensure each phase goes as smoothly as possible so you and your implementation team build integrity with your remote colleagues. Pay attention to the details and keep the public optics in mind. I once led a global support team during a very tricky international rollout. The implementation group was based in Boston, as was I. Unsurprisingly, our

Asian colleagues expressed reluctance to participate because they were convinced no one would support them properly due to the excessive time zone difference. I chose to provide live, real-time video support online so I could visibility represent the company with my Asian Pacific (APAC) colleagues during their business hours. I coordinated my work with a local Asian-based subject matter expert who provided logistical support during routine business hours. I provided her with all the recent updates that had occurred in Boston, so she always had the most recent up-to-date information. That helped her look good with her team during the Asian workday. Since my time zone was 13 hours behind APAC, I scheduled late night office hours to liaise with my APAC colleagues and collect their feedback. I'd bring the APAC feedback to our Boston technical team so they could complete technical revisions while our Asian colleagues slept. We did this for an entire year. Yes, it was a lot of extra work. But it was important to make a point and show solidarity and sincere respect for our colleagues overseas as no one had ever done that for them before. As a result, we gained credibility and good will that made future rollouts easier in that part of the world a whole lot easier because we had a personal history of mutual respect.

Highlights

Leverage pilots to test your plan

- Pilot projects are a cost-effective way to test new operational practices under controlled circumstances.
- Pilots help you introduce a change to a small group to provide proof of concept while building political support for and engagement in your new remote work operating model.
- Choose your pilot group with care as they will become your implementation team as you roll out the new model.

Build a network of remote work experts

- Look for experts inside and outside the company to support your pilot.
- Create a candidate profile indicating key characteristics you need to supplement the team.
- Recruit from all areas of the company as you need a multi-disciplinary team.
- Build your plan for training your team so they can support future phases of the rollout past the initial pilot.

Recruit engaged executive sponsors

- Organize a steering committee comprised of senior executives from multiple disciplines to help expedite decision making and help drive adoption for your new remote work operating model.

Collect and analyze data to measure progress

- Data, when used properly, tells a compelling story that can support your pilot work and help you build momentum for future phases of your rollout past your initial pilot.
- Choose the data that is most relevant for each stage of your implementation and for each audience you are addressing.

Create a robust reporting process

- Not all data is equal, identify the data that provides the best business intelligence, so you have clear, objective, realistic indicators of the success of your plans.
- Establish a baseline to measure against.
- In existing businesses use historic data to evaluate operational changes that result from adopting remote work but make sure you set up data equivalents, so you compare apples to apples.
- Reports are business tools. Resist report overload. Keep reports actionable and relevant, so they are an effective business tool for running your business.

Expand the rollout past the pilot

- Before your pilot ends, map out a phased approach to continue your rollout in a systematic and organized way.
- If you choose your future phase targets in advance, then keep them updated and fully informed during the pilot, it's easier to recruit them for future phases.
- It's a positive sign when colleagues come to you and volunteer to participate.
- It's easier to recruit volunteers when you have an organized support plan in place that has gained operational integrity through smooth execution.
- When your implementation involves drastic time differences, you have a chance to show respect by adjusting your work schedule to match the time zone that needs your support.

Note

1. https://www.ted.com/talks/derek_sivers_how_to_start_a_movement

Chapter 10

Managing Change

As a remote work professional working with real businesses to operationalize new ideas, managing change is constantly top of mind for me. My work has taught me it matters little how good the plan, the tool, the idea, the process is if no one will buy into it and adopt it. The data supports this as team resistance and lack of user adoption are the top two reasons change initiatives fail. That's why I've devoted a whole chapter to change management, but honestly, I'm just presenting a few fundamentals for you to consider. I could write an entire book on the topic of change management and remote team multi-channel communications because of the key roles they play in an implementation's success or failure.

Never, ever underestimate how much most people hate change. There are lots of logical, illogical, and emotional reasons for this that I'll discuss in this chapter. But while change aversion is powerfully real, there will always be someone you can count on who will see change as an energizing, interesting opportunity. You must take all this into consideration when you build your implementation plan if you want your remote work rollout to be a success. If change intimidates you or operationalizing stuff is new to you, don't worry. I'm going to lay out the steps I take to plan for, manage, and navigate change. Some things may seem a little counterintuitive to you at first, but trust me when I tell you, these techniques work. In this chapter, I discuss the need to:

- LISTEN: conduct a listening tour and shop your ideas
- EXPLAIN THE "WHY": shape the narrative
- OVER COMMUNICATE: share information freely
- RECRUIT: focus on the convertibles
- CELEBRATE: recognize, reward, and acknowledge
- STAY ALERT: assess, iterate, adapt, and pay attention to warning signs

DOI: 10.4324/9781003243557-10

LISTEN: Conduct a Listening Tour and Shop Your Ideas

Early on, as you develop your ideas and formulate your remote work plan, it's important to seek out other opinions as quickly as you can. If you create a plan by yourself or in isolation with a few others, you start to close yourself off from vital information. You get wedded to your initial ideas before you have all the facts. If there is no one to push back or challenge you, you assume your solution is perfect and you miss a precious opportunity to gain important operational data from a variety of subject matter experts. You also give up a chance to gain early buy-in and to surface employee and stakeholder concerns. As buy-in is critical, overlooking this step will come back to bite you badly later on down the line. If you are a highly logical person, change will challenge your perceptions in so many ways. If something seems logical to you, you may assume it is obviously logical to everyone else impacted by your plan. It's not. Never apply logic to an illogical situation and change work is much more emotionally driven than logically driven.

Every human has a particular tolerance for and reaction to change. However, they see it, their orientation toward change seems highly logical and completely justified to them personally. I like to call this emotional logic. This is an important concept because everyone I have ever interviewed about their reaction to change has some seemingly plausible reason for their response. It's also true that people get used to stuff over time when faced with gradual exposure. It's the frog in the boiling water story. If you dump a frog into boiling water, they jump out. Put them in room temperature water and add heat gradually and they sit tight. The first time an employee hears the words – "We are announcing a new initiative," they get triggered. Their instinctual response to change will kick in and I guarantee, a bunch of those employees are going to see this new initiative as a pot of boiling water and react accordingly.

There is also a very real emotional component to a human's reaction to change that tracks closely to a seemingly disconnected life event – grief. That's why I often use the Kubler-Ross' Five Stages of Grief[1] as an instructional tool to prepare implementation teams for what is about to happen during a remote work implementation rollout and it's the reason, I'm walking you through these changes steps to ensure your remote work rollout is a success. For those of you unfamiliar with Dr. Kubler-Ross, she was a Swiss-American psychiatrist who wrote a seminal book in 1969 called On Death and Dying.[2] In it, she introduced the distinct emotions humans experience at the end of life or when faced with a significant life-changing event – denial, anger, bargaining, depression, and acceptance.

Ironically, humans facing change in the workplace experience many of these emotions, thus you need to prepare to deal with them if you are implementing a big change. Your teams, even committed change lovers, will experience a range of emotions during the rollout process. By adopting this "drip" approach that gradually introduces the change through one-on-one conversations, pilot programs, and the other techniques I discuss in this chapter, you can anticipate and plan for these emotions and address them proactively in your roll out plan. Allocating time at the beginning of your planning process to schedule meetings with a variety of different people to hear their thoughts, opinions, and ideas is a great way to start.

This initial listening period allows you to ask questions that introduce new ideas without making the idea immediately official. That's a lot less intimidating than an official kickoff announcement or an email telling everyone they can expect a system upgrade tomorrow. It's a soft launch rather than a dictate. This improves your chances of gaining people's trust later when you need it as you have solicited their input and taken it into consideration ahead of time. Structure these listening meetings with intention. Formulate a short list of open-ended questions, then prepare to ask them without tone. Your goal is to gain as much information as possible as you introduce an idea through your carefully crafted question.

You will also get to take a pulse check on the level of resistance you are up against as you witness people's emotional reaction to the idea. Stay open-minded and resist the urge to argue or defend. Just listen and learn. When formulating your questions, there is no need to direct the conversation or push your ideas. Use the questions to introduce a topic – like remote work – without offering a specific plan. Just put the idea out there and see what happens. Sample a wide variety of people at several levels of the organization. It's important you keep things as neutral as possible. Here are a few sample questions to get you started:

- I'm exploring ways for us to better support our colleagues that work outside of our home office. Do you have any team members who work outside the home office? If so, what supports do you currently have in place to help them succeed?
- Is your team using digital work tools to communicate and get work done?
- Are you currently allowing flexible work schedules, if so, how is it working? If not, would you consider implementing flexible work options for your team?
- Do you or would you consider using video for team meetings and client meetings? Why or Why not?
- Have you or any of your team members worked from home at any time? If so, how is it working? If not, would you consider implementing work from home options for your team?

- As a company, are we currently able to technically support flexible work schedules?
- Do we currently have HR policies in place to accommodate flexible work programs here at our company?
- Is there anyone else you recommend I speak to that may have thoughts on this topic?
- If I have additional questions in the future, do you mind if I contact you again?

Listening tours are a casual way to start a low-risk dialogue with a broad audience. They give you intel that you can use to strategically build a strong business case to proactively promote your rollout. Plan your tour as soon as you can as it will provide many positive advantages. The operative word is "listening." You will need to give people a brief context for your questions so be prepared to frame the reason for your question or the person getting questioned will be guarded and suspicious. Give the context first, ask the question, then still back and listen to the respondent's answer. Listen for the obvious and pay attention to the subtext. Early on in your planning process, this activity helps you surface objections, evaluate change resistance levels, and measure reactions to an idea well before any implementation work begins.

Use your listening tour as a recruiting tour as you begin building a change coalition to support your future implementation plan. Asking questions helps you get an idea out in the open to get people thinking and talking in a less emotional way. This is what I call "shopping" an idea to get people used to it. It's the moment I turn on the burner gently and quietly at first. It's a great way to gauge someone's suitability for my change team and often I am planting a quiet seed so I can formally recruit them in the future. Shopping an idea tie directly to my discussions in earlier chapters on recruiting a remote work implementation team, identifying critical stakeholders, and utilizing an executive steering committee to sponsor and support your rollout. It's an important change management activity as it allows you to open a dialogue with a lot less emotion because the stakes are so low at this stage.

Introducing an early-stage idea also helps you formulate and practice your plan narrative as you gather vital information that will result in a better roll out. It's a chance to get conversations going, get people thinking, build trust, and familiarize people with the coming change. I call this a "drip campaign." It's a quiet way to normalize an idea through gentle repetition and ongoing low-level discussion. Some people get anxious about talking up an idea too early because they are worried it will promote group resistance. In my experience, it has the exact opposite effect. Withholding information, catching people unaware will cause far more emotional reactions, undermine trust, create unnecessary disruptions, a potential loss of momentum, and many hurt feelings. When people get caught off guard, they tend to jump to conclusions and think the worst. They feel you are hiding something, and they question your honesty. They lose trust and are much more likely to resist. No one likes surprises, particularly in the workplace because work is tied to people's livelihood, professional identity, and feeling of self-worth. Taking the time to have quiet one-on-one chats, shopping your idea through normal conversations, and listening carefully to each response may seem like a lot of work, but I promise you, it will speed things up over time and it will help you learn a lot while you get people used to the idea. So don't stay quiet, go on your listening tour and shop away!

EXPLAIN THE "WHY": Shape the Narrative

Stories are a powerful way to convey information and familiarize people with your plans. Earlier in this handbook in Chapter 2, I stressed the importance of identifying a clear end goal for your remote work operating model. Base your narrative on this goal. Prepare to communicate a clear vision of what the plan will achieve and why it's necessary. Keep it simple and practice it so you can repeat the vision over and over to everyone you meet. Outline the "whys" behind the move to remote work and layout the reasons for and benefits of the change. Be honest and positive. Test out the narrative as you conduct your listening tour and use it as a selling tool to recruit your implementation team and enlist stakeholder support. Once your implementation team is formed, expose them to the narrative so they can share it. Provide as many visible reminders of the narrative as you can and keep them out in public, so they are visible and supportive of your roll out "story." Often during implementations of this sort, I name the initiative and then distribute branded swag – coffee mugs, pens, pins, jackets, bags – as they are tangible symbols of the program, and they get people talking. All these things, the narrative, the why, the swag, work in unison to amplify the change message and give it power.

Proactively crafting the narrative allows you to positively control the initial project messaging and when your narrative is good and logical, it reduces people's anxiety. Remember you must plan for lots of emotions throughout your roll out. While everyone on the team will have their own reaction to any change you suggest, creating a strong, compelling rationale for your plan helps early adopters and reasonable skeptics to understand the logic behind the strategy and see the value of the change. Avoid making your narrative complicated. One example of a great narrative was developed by a client of ours, a national insurance company with a widely dispersed team. When we rolled out a new flexible work program, the company explained the goal was "to extend all the benefits of the company's friendly, people-centric culture to everyone on the team, regardless of where they worked."

In another instance, I worked with a Toyota corporate team to develop a change initiative focused on incenting US Toyota Dealers to re-tool their business models to account for changing consumer behavior. The existing dealer model relies too heavily on face-to-face customer interaction in a world now more comfortable buying a vehicle online and Toyota understands this is a looming business risk. But car dealers are all independent business owners who are reluctant to change. The Toyota corporate team presented their change narrative to their dealer community this way, "Toyota plans fifty years in advance, so we are prepared to adjust to market changes and we know we'll be ok. As we value our Dealer colleagues and wish them continued success as well, we are investing in this new initiative to help you re-tool your business operating models to incorporate more digital interactions, so you remain successful long term as well." Finally, at my company, the Remote Nation Institute, we are redefining and standardizing leadership practices that support and enable respectful, productive remote work. At my other company, Sophaya, we help our clients operationalize remote work and optimize engagement in remote teams. Ultimately, we are doing all of this to elevate the profile of remote professionals by building a Remote Nation community that celebrates remote work, supports those that do it, and promotes its untapped business value. That's the "why" that helps us inform our students, clients, and critical stakeholders of our mission and vision.

Throughout an implementation it's the consistency, repetition, and frequency of the narrative as well as the voices of the people who tell it – both formally and informally – that shape the credibility of any implementation story. Think of the way rumors spread, moving organically from person to person over different channels. Imagine your story is connected by a thread and your goal is to get the thread into as many hands as possible without breaking it or reshaping it. Keep your story simple and consistent. Make sure it addresses the typical questions any reasonable person would ask so you present the answers before anyone has to ask. Then, as you are presented with new questions, continue to adjust your narrative accordingly.

Examples of questions that are top-of-mind for anyone experiencing change in the workplace:

- Why are we making the change?
- Why is the change necessary at this time?
- How will this change impact me?
- Do I have to participate in this change?
- What benefit can I expect of the change?
- How will this change my job?

- Are there opportunities for me as a result of this change?
- Will this impact my pay or benefits?
- How will the company support me during and after this change?

OVER COMMUNICATE: Share Information Freely

When change is happening, there is always speculation and innuendo. Remember that gossip is inevitable whenever humans gather together. In the absence of positive information or real facts, people assume the worst, then change resistors to get control of the narrative and things can get ugly. Your listening tour and sharing your narrative will help you get ahead of the rumors and the gossip. But that won't be enough. Your listening tour introduces the idea and gets people talking, yes, but it also starts them wondering. The reason your narrative is important is it sets the tone and provides a context for the change and, hopefully, allows people to see where they fit into the future vision the narrative presents. Then consistent repetition and frequent positive messaging delivered by a variety of credible sources – you, your implementation team, your sponsors, and your stakeholders – start to add weight and authority to the rollout plan. I see a lot of people skip these steps then get themselves in trouble because change resisters become the dominant voices. In the absence of information, people make stuff up and I guarantee you whatever story they come up with is far more negative and destructive, so put in the effort to stay out ahead of things. Invest time and effort. It's well worth it. Work with your team and consult change experts to develop a comprehensive roll out communication plan to combat negative talk.

Recognizing information has a power dynamic to it. Depending on where someone sits in the hierarchy of an organization, signifies their status of importance. Use this to your advantage and share information strategically with key players, early adopters, and critical stakeholders so they feel special, then start spreading custom messages around through as many channels as possible. Don't "black-box" the rollout activities. Shout them from the rooftops as often as you can but do it with purpose and intent. Use updates, reports, town halls, prerecorded videos, team meetings, board meetings, whatever venues are available to you to spread the word. I understand this can feel intimidating, but it's necessary and a great way to hone your presentation skills.

I once had to deliver a roll out update to a global audience via video. That doesn't seem like that big of a deal except in this case, I had to stand on a 35-foot podium overlooking a trading floor full of investment bankers. The trading floor was in full operation, with lots of noise and activity. The space was the size of several football fields, and it was surrounded by 20 jumbotron video screens mounted all around the room, so I was visible to everyone, and all the traders had me in their line of sight from their work areas. I could see my face everywhere. My 15-minute update was simulcast globally across the world while I stood alone on top of the podium with my headset, microphone, and my PowerPoint slideshow. It was quite an experience and it taught me a lot.

Share the good stuff and the bad stuff so you present a balanced, realistic view to everyone concerned. Update everyone on the bad stuff as soon as possible so they hear it from you rather than the grapevine or, worse, a change resistor with a negative agenda. Put the roll out communication plan, the implementation team reporting structure, and the other logistical stuff I've discussed in this handbook in place early. Then set the expectations up front as to how you and the team will keep everyone informed in good times and bad. When something unexpected happens or a crisis occurs (plan for it, because it will), make sure your corresponding updates include the steps you are taking to mitigate the damage and get things back on track.

Stakeholders and sponsors don't like to be caught off guard. They want the facts and the plan. My update format with them is concise and to the point – just giving you a heads up, there's been some issues, here's what they are, here's what they mean, here's how they affect things, and here's what we're doing about them. With employees, I use a version of this format but add more concrete details pertaining to their specific circumstances. Then I follow-up and keep folks informed so they aren't guessing, and they see I'm on top of things. Think of all of this as a part of your drip campaign. The goal is to normalize information sharing with a proactive, steady flow that is consistent, proactive, strategic, and shows you are ready for anything.

If there is a problem, an operational misstep or a mistake made, own it. Acknowledge it fast, communicate the course of action, and fix it quickly all while keeping people informed. People are smart enough to expect occasional disruptions during a roll out, but people mind less if there is a swift, effective action plan with meaningful follow-through to rectify things. When the inevitable problem occurs, do not waste any time finding fault. The moment of crisis is no time to point fingers or worry about who is at fault. Fix the damn problem, then debrief after the crisis has passed, learn the lessons, remediate, when necessary, incorporate learnings, and move on. Period. Anticipate there will be problems, plan for them, create a rollout support plan that is communicated well in advance and is visible to anyone immediately impacted by your roll out plan. This means you and your team must keep close to the action, so you can get ahead of the message BEFORE it gets out of control. Doing this is simple if you develop trusted relationships with the employees impacted by each phase of your rollout and you provide ample roll out resources who keep an eye on the impacts of the roll out in real time.

Communicating today is easier but more complex than ever. Given the advances in technology, I no longer have to stand on a podium to transmit a video message, I have lots more choices. I can easily pre-record a video or audio message, send a digital update, or jump on a live stream video conferencing platform for a real time question and answer session. In Chapter 11, I'll go into more detail on the strategic use of digital channels and talk about the pros and cons of multi-channel communications during remote work implementation roll outs.

RECRUIT: Focus on the Convertibles

During implementation projects it's easy to get caught up fighting people's resistance to change. I know it may seem counter intuitive, but resistors are not your problem, rather they are a distraction that will sap your resources and slow your momentum if you let them. Don't waste any time trying to convert people who are against change. Rather, shift your tactics and focus on building your coalition of early adopters first. Everything I have outlined in this handbook will help you do this. Your goal is to create forward momentum by recruiting change advocates and early adopters who show interest and are energized by change. In Derek Sivers' 2010 TED talk: How to start a movement[3] Sivers visually demonstrates how to build a coalition in a three-minute video that visually shows the difference those first few followers can make. Start with people who say yes to the change – early adopters, open-minded skeptics, people who see it as a career advantage, or individuals who will join in because they trust you. Present this group to others as the face of the change. Make them project leaders, spokespeople, and present them as visible change champions. Choose them strategically. Seek respected people of good standing with some visibility in the organization and employees in good standing who are recognized experts at their jobs.

Once these folks join the implementation team, assign them visible roles, and get them working as process testers, trainers, subject matter experts, and project managers. Initially you'll find it necessary to "sell" your idea to these first few recruits. As things start to shift, people will come to you to ask to be part of the change. That's when things pivot, and you know you've made progress. Understand you will never convert everyone. You don't have to, all you need is critical mass and positive, forward momentum. Once your implementation reaches a critical tipping point where the majority of the company employees accept and adopt the change, resistors will feel greater social pressure to conform. At this stage, it becomes more costly for people to resist. Even then, there will be holdouts, but they are easier to manage as they are now the minority, the outliers, and they stick out like sore thumbs. It's hard for them to hide. They will either give up and convert themselves grudgingly, self-select out and find employment elsewhere, or, if they are disruptive and unprofessional, you can manage them out using the Leader-Led accountability cycle and your disciplinary process.

CELEBRATE: Recognize, Reward, and Acknowledge

Celebration, recognition, and sharing credit are lovely ways to publicly acknowledge everyone participating in the rollout – your implementation team, stakeholders, your executive steering committee, the pilot group, and any early adopters are a good place to start. Build celebration and acknowledgement into your communication plan and make it a routine part of your process to recognize the people you work with every day. Share success stories in reports, newsletters, town halls, and whenever you present updates, give lots of credit to everyone you can whenever you can. As the rollout expands to new parts of your company, continue to publicly recognize participants for their efforts. Celebrations signal the implementation is moving forward successfully. Positive reinforcement is such a nice way to give credit where credit is due. This keeps your project visible, positive, and top-of-mind.

It's true that some people will work harder than others and some people will contribute more than others but don't be stingy with praise for even the smallest effort. Use positive reinforcement as a coaching tool to catch people doing things right so they gain confidence and start to see the value of the change. One of the reasons people resist change is the loss of capability and expertise as they give up their old ways. Change means learning new things and during that learning curve, it means making mistakes and looking less competent. Adults are particularly sensitive to this loss of status as they learn and often, they resist learning because they feel stupid or inept. By providing positive feedback, you can alleviate some of their discomfort and give them the confidence they need to keep going until they get it right. As a change management tool, driving adoption by acknowledging people for getting onboard with the new remote work operations model is not only a smart tactic, but also a great way to lift people's spirits as they adjust to their new normal. There are so many ways to do this, be generous and have fun with it.

When you share credit, do it strategically, but sincerely. Alert senior executives of their team's successes so the executive can feel satisfaction in their people's success. Share achievements up through the food chain from new employees to line staff to the highest levels. Telling someone they are great is one thing, telling someone's boss they are great is even better as it provides the boss with valuable information. If that information comes from you, it has more weight especially if it comes unsolicited. It will make a welcome change as every manager hears when something goes wrong, yet they rarely hear about the good stuff. Focus on positive messaging in all your communications. Give specific examples and tie it to actual performance outcomes. This gives people the positive lift they need to continue with the hard work of operationalization and institutionalizing the new way.

This is important as change is hard and anything that adds energy and lifts people's spirits makes the work easier for everyone. Make sure the praise is tied to a performance action, be specific, and timely in how and when you deliver the praise. Finally, whether you are upgrading or transforming an existing operating model or building something new, I recommend you invest heavily in your leaders to ensure they are prepared to adjust their styles to coaching in support of the Leader-Led accountability cycle I discussed in Chapter 6. If your leaders, managers, and supervisors insist on using old methodologies like command and control, hierarchical leadership methods, micro-management, or they rely on in-person leadership approaches, team trust will suffer and building a healthy, positive team culture will be next to impossible.

STAY ALERT: Assess, Iterate, Adapt, and Pay Attention to Warning Signs

Planning things out conceptually is exciting and it makes things seem so easy. Implementing and operationalizing your plan is a hell of a lot of work full of twists and turns. Nothing ever goes exactly as planned so stay alert. When you are an existing operation, integrating old systems and new systems is way harder than anyone will admit. Old technology and new tech don't play nice together regardless of what the sales rep says. Even the smallest change can have major downstream impacts and create monumental chaos. Don't skimp on your implementation budget and try to recruit skilled implementers who know your company and understand change management. Poor implementations create a lot of dissent and give your dissenters a lot of ammunition to use against you. The smoother the rollout process goes, the easier it is for you to gain additional buy-in for your long-term vision. Make your plan, then prepare to adjust, shift, transform, adapt to everything that rears its ugly head throughout the process. Then take the lessons learned in each crisis, apply them, and get better next time. That's how you build trust with your teams.

In remote teams, trust is important, but even your most trusted people can't anticipate everything so it's best to be extra careful and explicitly check and double check each milestone along the way. This is particularly important in large remote teams as the further afield someone is, the less urgency they feel to comply unless they really feel engaged, and the more reluctant they are to admit they are in trouble. I found this out the hard way very early in my remote work career. At the time, I was based in Boston when I was put in charge of a large international implementation. I was anxious to succeed as, at that time, it was my biggest assignment of my career. My team and I had worked for months, planning out every detail. We selected our first rollout site – London. I had traveled to the location several times to make sure the local team had the information and the support they needed to launch on schedule. During my London visits, my gut told me the local manager wasn't onboard, but I ignored the warning signs as I assumed incorrectly, that she would get onboard in the end. Instead, I listened to our local contact, an enthusiastic young woman, who kept telling me the system was configured as requested and her boss was supportive. But I didn't push, and I didn't verify.

Although the local manager continued to seem to send signals she was disengaged and uninterested, everything seemed to be on track according to my local contact. I naively assumed everything was ready to go. It was quite a lesson on go-live day when I discovered to my horror and shame that the London manager called my boss, yelled a lot, pulled rank, and refused to let the rollout proceed as planned. While I was working with her team, she was working behind the scenes to get support from senior executives to stop the roll out plan because she didn't like the change. She was always careful and cordial to my face, but behind my back she completely ruined me. It took me several months of late nights and backtracking to put things right and in the end, we completed the rollout and eventually gained buy-in for the plan from the London group, but it was not without cost to me and, temporarily, my professional reputation. I learned a hard, but valuable, lesson that day and after I recovered, I took those lessons to heart and as a result, I've never experienced anything like that happening again (thank goodness!).

Here's what I learned because of that terrible experience: Keep your stakeholders informed and be clear who those stakeholders are at all times. Remember as your implementation expands and rolls out to new areas, there are probably new stakeholders that need attention well before the local go-live date. Take time to identify them and connect with them early so you control the narrative and information they get. This is a predictable cycle for each new phase of your implementation roll out plan. Create a checklist for yourself to follow as the roll out expands from one part of your organization to another. I've given you a base framework to get you started, customize yours according to your unique circumstances.

Creating a Regional Readiness Activities Checklist

My list is by no means comprehensive, but it gives you a starting point. Add due dates for each of these activities so you formulate a working timeline that you can share with your team and the local team. Once you have a detailed roll out timeline template, keep tweaking it as you learn more, so each phase of the roll out gets smoother and more organized. This will help as the later phases of the roll out will include more change resisters and the smoother the roll out, the less ammunition they have to use against you.

- Contact regional executives well ahead of any roll out activities and schedule a meeting to provide them with an overview of the roll out objectives and tell them what to expect and what you need from them to ensure a smooth roll out.
- Negotiate with regional executives to identify a roll out schedule that is the least operationally disruptive.
- Establish a go-live date based on the time it will take the implementation team and the local team to execute all the operational preparation tasks leading up to the go-live moment.
- Use the pilot project as a baseline to estimate time needed to complete tasks but interview your local contacts to determine if there are unique variables e.g., different digital tools, lack of consistent internet, local regulatory factors, unique workflows, or business system requirements that may impact the roll out timeline.
- Count back from the go-live date and schedule implementation activities starting from today and leading up to the selected go-live date.
- Make sure the calendar provides sufficient time to fully complete implementation activities.
- Keep the timeline tight but realistic.[4]
- Have regional executives designate a regional point of contact to work with your implementation team during the roll out.
- Work with the regional executive to get the word out about the upcoming roll out. Follow the hierarchy so executives, leaders, managers, supervisors know first, then do a broad-based communication to the entire group.
- Invest in building these relationships, meet with the local teams often and have your implementation team leader do the same. I usually negotiated with the regional executives to attend their regular management meetings periodically, so they always know what is coming next and they get used to working with me.[5]
- Create a master roll out activities schedule that includes all the elements we've covered in this handbook.
- Schedule local team training early on so the local team has time to experience the new processes and workflows.
- Include pilot activities that were well received.
- Incorporate your communication plans.
- Incorporate your support plan leading up to go-live day.

Invest in building local stakeholder relationships so there is trust and respect. Even though I took a beating in this one instance, I don't let that experience influence my approach. I always give everyone the benefit of the doubt up front. However, I am careful to set up clear accountability by clarifying expectations, then follow-up consistently. Trust, but verify, that's my motto. When someone tells you everything is fine, and work is complete, ask for verifiable proof of completion, then double check. There is an old saying – people expect what you inspect. Hold routine check-ins, schedule practice runs, and review specific evidence of progress with your team and all stakeholders, especially the ones most impacted at the time of go-live. Then trust your instincts and investigate immediately if things don't seem right so you can catch issues early on before they become a real problem.

Everyone knows rollouts have their bumps and bruises. Prepare for problems as best you can, build a strong rollout support plan, stay vigilant, and when problems do occur, stay calm and professional, focus on solving rather than blaming or finding fault, and fix things quickly. Adjust, adjust, adjust. Tweak as needed, internalize the lessons you learn, and don't let ego get in the way. There are a lot of voices in remote work implementations and each participant will have their preferences and advocate for their "way." As I mentioned early in this handbook, it's important to have an experienced implementation leader that can look at the big picture and provide a balanced perspective. The implementation leader must weigh the pros and cons of an issue then provide a cohesive way forward based on the agreed upon business goals, timelines, and deliverables. All that planning you did at the beginning will now come into play as your vision, mission, values, and business goals become the guide markers for implementation choices.

Highlights

LISTEN: conduct a listening tour and shop your ideas
 EXPLAIN THE "WHY": shape the narrative

- Stories are a powerful way to convey information and share the plan.
- Start with the goals, mission, and vision we discussed earlier in this handbook.
- Craft a story that addresses the "why" behind the change that aligns with the end goals.
- Keep it simple and teach it to the implementation team so they can share it with others.
- Share the good stuff and the bad stuff – be honest and transparent, then indicate how you will fix the problem.

OVER COMMUNICATE: share information freely

- In the absence of information, people make things up and what they make up is never helpful to your roll out.
- Your listening tour and narrative are two ways you can present a positive alternative for your employees impacted most by the change.
- Use physical items like coffee mugs, pens, t-shirts, pins, jackets, bags that are branded with your change message reinforce your narrative in a fun, visible way.
- Recognizing information has a powerful dynamic, so share information strategically with intent and purpose.
- Senior leaders, stakeholders, and sponsors dislike surprises, and keep them informed at all times.
- When a mistake occurs, and it will happen, let people know quickly and provide your mitigation plan.
- Invest time up front to create a robust communication plan that supports your remote work implementation plan, then apply it consistently and thoughtfully throughout the roll out.

RECRUIT: focus on the convertibles

- While it may seem counter intuitive, don't waste time trying to convert resisters.
- Focus on the convertibles that see the opportunity in the change and recruit them for your implementation team.
- Once you have your implementation team, give them roles, and put them to work.
- Watch for the moment when people start coming to you asking about the rollout. This is an indicator the rollout is at a critical turning point with positive forward momentum.

CELEBRATE: recognize, reward, and acknowledge

- Celebrate, recognize achievements, and acknowledge effort whenever you can.
- Be strategic, but sincere and positive.
- Acknowledge employee efforts, then alert their boss as well so the boss can thank the employee as well.
- Whether the effort is big or small, don't be stingy with your praise.
- Maintaining a positive tone gives people the energy they need to do the hard work.
- Make sure to invest in your leaders so they are ready to adopt new leadership approaches that support a positive and healthy remote work culture.

STAY ALERT: assess, iterate, adapt, and pay attention to warning signs

■ Nothing ever goes according to plan so stay alert and be prepared to adjust.
■ Create a master roll out checklist that helps standardize the roll out practices and allows the implementation team to get better over time.
■ The smoother the rollout goes, the easier it is to maintain rollout momentum.
■ Keep a close eye on things during the rollout, address problems quickly, and apply the lessons learned immediately.
■ Maintain trust with your team by keeping everyone informed.
■ Trust, but verify, to ensure there is accountability in each phase of your rollout.
■ As you expand your rollout to new parts of the company, identify the local stakeholders and connect with them early.
■ Trust your instincts, if you sense something is wrong, check it out and ask for verification.

Notes

1. Kübler-Ross E, Kessler D (2014). *On Grief and Grieving: Finding the Meaning of Grief Through the Five Stages of Loss.* New York: Scribner. ISBN 978-1476775555. OCLC 863077888
2. Kübler-Ross E (1969). *On Death and Dying.* New York: The Macmillan Company. ISBN 0026050609
3. Derek Sivers: How to start a movement, https://www.ted.com/talks/derek_sivers_how_to_start_a_movement
4. There is nothing worse than implementation timelines with arbitrary go-live dates that everyone knows are unachievable. Having unrealistic timelines does not motivate a team nor does it create a useful sense of operational urgency. Rather, it creates an adversarial partner dynamic that lets people down, fosters resentment, hurts you and the implementation team's credibility, and discourages everyone.
5. Since these are the decision makers, having a good rapport with them, makes it easier to reach consensus and gain buy-in.

Chapter 11

Multi-Channel Communications

Effective communication skills, verbal, written, and digital, are fundamental to remote work success. Communication today is complicated because of all the technology options available today. Things are very channelized, and everyone has their digital preferences. Since there are multiple channels, people can miss messages. This is particularly true if the message is sent via a channel the receiver does not use or can't access. If the message is ignored or missed, the communication loop isn't completed, and the person sending the message ends up frustrated and talking to themselves. This is a formula for disaster in dispersed teams as unread, missed, or ignored messages create an adversarial team dynamic, break down team trust, and foster frustration and conflict.

In earlier chapters I addressed the need for remote teams to develop communication protocols and that will help alleviate some of these problems. In this chapter I'm going to provide some basic multi-channel communication fundamentals that can support your implementation roll out and help with communication among your implementation team. I am barely scratching the surface here. Like change management, I could write a whole book on remote team communications as poor communication and a lack of understanding of today's ever-evolving multi-channel environment is another key reason remote teams fail to build positive team cultures and achieve top productivity.

Even if you think you are a good communicator, things are changing SO rapidly and are now very generational, challenge your assumptions, and examine your communication approaches in this new remote workplace. This is an area, like technology, which is ever-changing and to stay effective you need to adapt and adjust to stay relevant. In this chapter, I'll outline the changes I've witnessed in team communications and explain how more traditional methods like handwritten notes are still relevant and helpful in certain circumstances. I'll also point out how they will seem antiquated and untrustworthy. I'll even discuss how emojis and emoticons add real value even in business communications depending on the audience, your business objectives, and the channel you use. I'm getting tactical and granular again as communication is such an essential, fundamental part of any implementation. Topics I cover include how to:

■ leverage the online to offline (O2O2O) communication flow
■ communication in remote teams works differently
■ build remote team communications systems then standardize them
■ create touchpoints that build remote team engagement
■ teach yourself and your people channel etiquette
■ recognize digital communication limits
■ reduce message distortion by connecting directly with your audience

Leverage the Online to Offline (O2O2O) Communication Flow

The flow of communication is different today and everyone is feeling the change. First, there's the sheer volume. Email inboxes are overflowing and as many of us have multiple email addresses to contend with we've started to prioritize what emails get our attention and which ones do not. Second, we work on multiple devices. Some of those devices are synced, and some are not. Some of those devices have small screens e.g., watches, cell phones, tablets and some come with jumbo screens that help us see each other and build rapport. Once, when I was working in Australia, we used a life-sized screen to virtually meet with our Japanese colleagues because we wanted to be able to show respect by starting each meeting bowing to each other virtually. It generated a lot of good will between the groups. Third, these devices are loaded with a million new apps and software tools that remote teams can use to connect, communicate, and do work together. Some of this software is device specific e.g., texting, while some software is accessible across all our devices.

If that isn't enough to confuse you, having a conversation these days has completely shifted from an episodic face-to-face interlude and periodic in-person interaction to something that is very different. Today a communication interaction is continual and extended. A business discussion may start online with an email that turns into a video or phone call that turns into a text message that turns back into an email that turns into a cup of coffee together in real life (IRL) or via video chat. As we fluidly switch from one channel to another, we continue

O2O2O Multi-Channel Communication Threads

Engagement and conversation in the digital age combines active, passive, and in-person channels in a fluid and continuous flow throughout the work day.

In-Person Interactions	Active Channels	Passive Channels
Team or one-on-one meetings, conferences	Video conferencing, SMS, phone calls, group discussion channels	Project management software, social media, discussion boards, blogs, podcasts

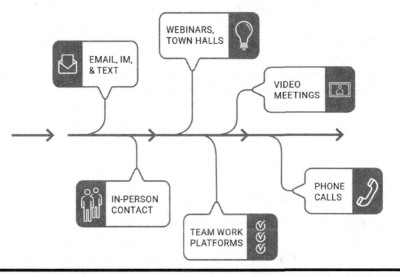

Figure 11.1 Used strategically, these O2O2O interactions can break down our natural suspicion of strangers and encourage familiarity and open contact among a remote team

to converse (sometimes non-stop) in one unending communication thread. I call this the O2O2O Effect (Figure 11.1)

This is the constant flow of information traveling through continual touch-points that move forward, sometimes actively, sometimes passively, from one channel to another. In this new construct, we maintain constant connection with people even though we may never meet them face-to-face. In remote teams, this is a valuable tool because each point of contact, each touchpoint, along the ongoing communication thread is an opportunity for remote team leaders and remote team colleagues to share information and build relationships in new and potentially positive, engaged ways. When used strategically, these O2O2O interactions can break down our natural suspicion of strangers and encourage familiarity and open contact among a remote team. It's like when a friend of yours keeps mentioning another friend of theirs so often that you start to feel like you know their friend vicariously through your association with your friend.

This is how social platforms work. We get a glimpse into the lives of people we have never met or vaguely know but we develop a sense of familiarity, even companionship with them, because of our experience of ongoing contact and passive exposure to their lives through shared content and our connection to our mutual friends. And while this may be more prevalent in younger professionals weaned on digital media and the internet, addiction to smartphones is multi-generational so this phenomenon is now the human condition streaming across generations. As technology continues to evolve and we continue to develop new stuff, communication will continue to morph and there will be opportunities for added business value, particularly in remote teams. However, on the flip side, this means whatever communication protocols, devices, and software you adopt will be obsolete the moment you deploy them. Prepare to adapt and plan for this for the foreseeable future.

Communication in Remote Teams Works Differently

The textbook definition of communication is the imparting or exchanging of information or news. Traditional communication models indicate a communication interaction as a cycle, a circular closed loop. The sender has an idea, they compose their message, deliver the message, then the receiver receives the message, interprets the message, and responds in some way. Face-to-face communication is very rich. It's multi-layered, nuanced, and contextual. The sender and receiver have many verbal and visual indicators; body language, tone of voice, facial expressions available to support the intention and the message. These non-verbal cues provide contextual clues to both parties as to the sender's state of mind when they sent the message and the reaction of the receiver indicating a) they got the message and b) what they think of it. Yet even in the best of circumstances when all parties are in the same room facing each other, misunderstands and communication breakdowns abound. As a species, we are remarkably bad at getting our point across.

When communication moves online and the people communicating are at a distance from each other, the communication dynamic changes. First, the

O2O2O Effect transforms messages into an ongoing, linear event that stays open and ongoing. Second, Remote teams are highly dependent on technology and the internet. Using digital channels for communicating is time efficient and seems easy, yet digital communication is tricky because most digital channels lack body language, and the message's recipient determines the tone and context of a message based on their state of mind when they receive the message and the nature of their relationship with the sender. Are you friend or foe? Third, there are also practical operational considerations that can disrupt or have unintended consequences e.g., lack of channel access, device problems, overly restrictive security protocols, or a lack of connectivity to the internet means the teams are unable to connect or get work done.

Effective communication in a remote team, dependent on digital tools, internet connectivity, and trust between distant parties, is much more complicated and far more likely to miss the mark. Remote team communication involves all the traditional communication methods plus any O2O2O linear communication interaction that takes place online and is composed and delivered via a device. Channel choice, device compatibility, internet connectivity, internet speed and bandwidth must align for remote communication to succeed in this multi-channel, remote work universe. Finally, there is the human factor. Since digital messaging has a flat affect, it is devoid of context. Messages lacking nonverbal cues are interpreted by the receiver based on their emotional state of mind and their relationship with the sender at the moment the message is opened. Presuming, of course, the receiver decides to or is able to access it and open it. So, this begs the question, if we send a digital message, an email, text, or instant message, are we *really* communicating? The answer is: only if the person receiving our digital message chooses to engage by opening it and responding to us. This works best and is more likely to happen if the sender and receiver have fully digital channel connectivity and enough trust between them to each give each other the benefit of the doubt.

This lack of context and tone results in lots of misunderstandings. Emojis and emoticons were invented as an attempt to provide a message sender the capability to add a visual indicator of their intended tone of voice. This only works when everyone understands this new language and interprets it as the sender intended. Smiley faces have limits as not everyone sees them as professional and generationally, different symbols mean different things. Also, different channels lend themselves to their use while others do not. So once again, having an agreed upon standard and accepted protocols is necessary if you want to avoid operational chaos.

In remote teams, it's all about trust. If you want to elevate your communication skills and become an effective multi-channel communicator, you must consciously work with your team and create the conditions, both

Remote Teams Need Dynamic, Reliable Information Flow to Thrive

Share information and listen to feedback using all the available channels to stay in touch and build trust.

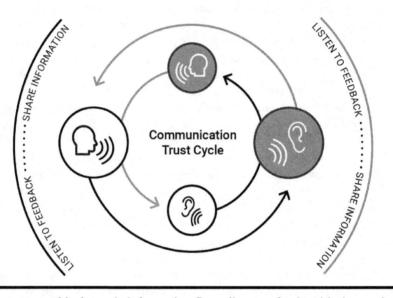

Figure 11.2   This dynamic information flow aligns perfectly with the Leader-Led Accountability Cycle, promoting team trust and positive team culture

technically and humanely, that support a culture of trust amongst your group that allows and rewards them for giving each other the benefit of the doubt. To do this, establish a dynamic flow of information (Fig. 11.2) between you and anyone you communicate with through regular contact and conscious information sharing. Since there is no "water-cooler" chat in remote teams, information sharing that goes both ways helps you do a wellness check-in to maintain the relationship and strengthen it. It's as important to listen as much as to share.

Not only does the information need to flow in both directions, but it also needs to be honest, transparent, and objective. This dynamic information flow aligns perfectly with the Leader-Led Accountability Cycle and the other elements I've covered in this handbook, and it feeds team trust and promotes a positive remote team culture. Leaders that actively employ this system are more likely to gain access to timely, honest information and remote employees are more likely to feel heard. Consider all the ways communications impact a business. It's such a crucial skill. I recommend any leader make remote multi-channel communication training a priority for themselves and their people. The return on investment (ROI) is huge. In the meantime, here are some basic rules to follow that will improve your chances of remote team communication success:

- Have a clear objective, a specific reason for your communication and craft your message accordingly.
- Be explicit about the message's purpose and include specific details – what you need, when you need it, why it's important, etc. so the recipient doesn't have to guess.
- Make it easy for the recipient to respond.
- Consider your audience carefully and craft your message for them, taking into consideration their preferences and your relationship and work history with them.
- Remember every communication is a touchpoint – include the facts but consider adding social niceties that acknowledge the human side of things.[1]
- Choose a channel that supports the message and is accessible and frequented by your intended audience.
- If you are using a digital channel, consider the channel etiquette and the limits of digital messaging.
- Avoid acronyms, jargon, or language specific to your discipline unless you know your intended audience understands the lingo.
- When communicating with an international or unknown audience, avoid slang or "localisms" specific to your region as they may be unknown and cause confusion.
- Think about when you are sending the message, not just your time zone, but the time zone of the recipient.
- Use "reply all" judiciously and don't fill up someone's mailbox unless it is absolutely necessary, and the recipient has agreed to it.
- Avoid using digital to resolve conflict or misunderstandings, pick up the phone, schedule a video call, or meet face-to-face (if possible). I'll get into this in more detail in the next sections, but trust me when I tell you, you should never fight online. It never ends well.

Build Remote Team Communication Systems then Standardize Them

Because the choice of tools these days is almost endless and the selection is growing every day, trying to build a cohesive, connected, productive remote team without a standardized, agreed upon process is an operations nightmare. It's likely to fail. As I've discussed, there are so many barriers to communication success and lots of room for misinterpretation in the best of circumstances. If every team member uses whatever they prefer things get confusing and break down fast. Multi-channel remote team communications are only effective when there is agreement on protocols and process, team buy-in, trust, mutual respect, and full team access and connectivity. There must be agreement that everyone will follow them appropriately. That's why it's essential for remote teams to come to some consensus as to the channels, work tools, interpersonal interaction protocols, and collaboration workflows they will use as a group to talk to each other, stay connected, and work together effectively as a team.

Problems occur when:

- Everyone picks their own channels, devices, platforms – chaotic, inefficient, and frustrating.
- Everyone is working in different time zones but as a group, they fail to make respectful accommodations, resentments can form quickly.
- The team is international and country standards for privacy, internet access, Wi-Fi bandwidth capabilities and internet accessibility vary.
- Technology systems aren't connected, or security protocols are so locked down that they disrupt workflow and the collaboration because they are too hard, and people give up (workaround proliferate and everyone circumvents the system).
- Technology doesn't keep up with the times.
- New employees, young and old, are allowed to apply their technology biases and they will bring unvetted software or personal devices in house without telling you.

You need one standard. Once you have one, seek user adoption of that standard, and then constantly monitor and update the standard as things change and new technology presents itself. I've found that it is easier to drive adoption of a standard if the team helps build it. Once the standard is crafted and in place, add it to the expectations shared with anyone joining the team, then incorporate it into your normal performance accountability feedback. This is how the Leader-Led Accountability Cycle provides you with the necessary operational framework to hold the team accountable for the standards they, themselves, set.

Create Touchpoints that Build Remote Team Engagement

There are so many ways for remote teams to connect and interact these days. But if you want to build meaningful engagement, think systemically. In each chapter of this handbook, I've outlined the components of a remote work operating model. How you build each component and infuse it with some cultural touch will help create a sense of shared community. The benefit of investing the time as you build out your plan, is the long-term paybacks. Infusing cultural touchpoints at all stages is the proper way to grow a remote team to top productivity and keep them there. In addition to the cultural elements built into your operating model, pay attention to your communication interactions. Stay cognizant that every interaction is a touchpoint. Don't waste any of them. Every operational element I've discussed in this handbook is a touch point that conveys who you are as a leader and what you stand for as a company. By providing an organized work environment that recognizes and values remote employees, you send a message. How you connect and communicate day in, and day out sends a message, too. Leveraging all the elements together, melding them and doing it with strategic purpose is when a remote team thrives.

When touchpoints are aligned together the team experiences the cumulative effect, the formation of a high functioning virtual office structure. How the touchpoints are executed by the leaders at your company will determine if that office structure has resilience, engenders respect, and supports a positive growth culture where people can learn and feel empowered. So, invest in remote leadership training that supports all that you have built. Tailor your touchpoints to meet the needs of your remote employees AND your business strategy so both can thrive. Use the 02020 Effect to create and share positive stories and develop fun people-to-people activities that embody your mission and values. Touchpoints tie everything together and strengthen your organization. They mold culture, support work efficiency, build trust, and elevate productivity. Don't squander them.

Teach Yourself and Your People Channel Etiquette

Once you figure out what digital tools you and your team will use, invest in team training to ensure everyone's understanding of the tool etiquette is in sync. Just like emojis and emoticons, there is lots of room for interpretation. Don't assume everyone uses digital tools the same. Consider this as you design your new hire training as generationally, we all see channels differently. Younger people are less familiar with email and may never have used it before coming to the workplace. Anyone joining the workplace these days grew up in a digital environment and are "digital natives." As a rule, they have a different orientation toward digital communications and little sense of traditional social hierarchy. I often hear my older clients complaining that young professionals overstep because they email senior leaders (as if this is a scandalous crime), or they prefer text to the phone, don't check voicemails, and use emojis in business communications. While older people are labeled by younger folks as technology and emoji resistant and wedded to old notions that remote work = slacking off.

To be clear, I don't want to generalize or pigeonhole anyone, as I know young people who are less technically inclined and older people who are highly digitally versant and who embrace change. Suffice it to say, it will save you a lot of headaches if you standardize the team's channel etiquette then stick to it, or at minimum have team discussions on the topic to discuss proper use. What is important is that any professional today prepares themselves for an ever-changing environment that will continue to evolve over time. We all must continue to educate ourselves to stay informed of what is relevant in the now. So, as I discuss channel etiquette, appreciate anything I say here has probably morphed in some way. Talk to your people to find out from them how they approach channel etiquette, so you have the latest perspective from the people using the channels in your workplace. With that disclaimer in mind, here are some examples of channel etiquette to consider:

Email

Email is the oldest and most conservative of the digital channels. There are many who view it as an antiquated, slow, outmoded tool yet it is still the business standard in most companies today. Email is a formal channel that lends itself to long-form messages, meeting recaps, and group messages. A sender can opt to assign flags to indicate a message's priority or request delivery and read receipts to ensure a message is viewed. As email is the most formal channel, there is a lot of debate about less formal tools like emojis and emoticons. Many of us have multiple emails and inbox maintenance is a huge burden. Because of the sheer volume of emails, to survive, we've become scanning culture, reviewing subject lines to decide if a message is a priority, or worthy of our attention. Since spammers and malware is more sophisticated these days, any email that looks suspicious gets deleted fast, it's easy for a message to get lost and go unseen.

Instant Messaging and Chat Functions

IM and chat are quick, informal channels usually included with today's work platforms. Generally, they are internal business forums for easy, instant access between work colleagues. They are great for asking quick questions, checking availability, providing quick updates, and sharing stuff.

Group Work Platforms

There has been a proliferation of teamwork platforms that act as virtual forums for all hands discussions, work team side groups, or one-on-one direct interactions. I have seen them used very effectively for a certain sized group when they are well moderated, and they are supported by defined forum etiquette. It takes a while for some people to get used to this free flow of information. Initially it's a bit like drinking from a fire hose. However, I've seen teams get into a lot of trouble with these forums if there aren't some basic rules. Like many online forums, rules can develop organically but that can be a drawback since, in the absence of established etiquette, louder voices can take control and use their influence to intimidate others. I've seen bullying and "bro" culture flourish in these channels with diversity of thought shutdown through group intimidation. These forums are also hard for new employees to navigate unless there is a formal introduction to a group.

Texting

Like IM and chat, texting is a short form, informal channel. But texting is different from IM and chat in significant ways. Generally, users are introduced to texting as a digital conversation tool outside of work through their personal cell phones. For many people, texting is a more intimate channel used with friends and family. So, there is sometimes an awkwardness when it moves into the workplace as it blurs an already blurred line between work time and personal time. As most young people are heavy text users, they are more likely to respond to a text than a phone call, yet for older people receiving a work text on a cell phone is an unacceptable invasion of privacy unless they have given their permission. So, tread lightly when using text, particularly if your people use their personal cell phones for business purposes. Get permission first, before assuming a text is an acceptable option.

Voicemail

No one picks up the phone anymore unless the call has been prearranged or the caller ID indicates the caller is a friend or family member. Many companies are evaluating their expensive landline systems, and some are abandoning landlines altogether. I see this as a continued trend with desk phones getting phased out over time.

Use of CC: and "Reply All"

Inbox volume is a genuine concern. In companies heavily reliant on email, CC: and "Reply All" are so prevalent that it's impossible sometimes to know what is relevant and what's not. I hear lots of people complaining how hard it is to discern priority and determine if a group message thread contains information that requires their attention. Think about how you use these features and, if you aren't getting the response you want, examine your email practices as your actions may be the root cause of your troubles.

There are lots more things I could write on this topic, but I will save that for another book. Suffice it to say, digital etiquette is worth your time and consideration. Invest time to choose the tools that best suit your business needs, establish some basic rules of engagement, hold yourself and your team accountable to them, and then evaluate frequently. If communication breakdowns happen frequently, examine your process, and find a fix before your remote team productivity suffers.

Recognize Digital Communication Limits

As time efficient and useful as digital communication is, it has limits. First, it does represent a legitimate business risk that we should all keep top of mind. Digital messages are an official business record and, as such, must be retained and archived just like tax documents. As it is an official record, it is also discoverable which means it may be used in legal proceedings in the event of some legal action. This included all digital channels – email, texting, instant messages (IM), cell phone calls, voice mails, etc. Since digital messages are digital, they are traceable and permanent. They can be shared easily with large groups of people and taken out of context for nefarious purposes. Today's cell phones contain GPS technology so they are trackable, microphones so they can record, cameras so they can take pictures. All this data is stored on the device and with cloud providers, so it is nearly impossible to eliminate data as everything is traceable. Messages that are posted on the internet, once shared, are no longer containable. All this poses a big security risk. I discussed some of this previously when I talked about IT security.

Second, digital speeds up people's response time and that means sometimes we hit send before we consider the impact or consequences of our message. When we are in the groove, moving through our day, feeling time pressed, and stressed out, it's easy to send a digital message rather than pick up the phone or schedule a video chat. Remote professionals can't afford to operate this way for long as this lack of consciousness and communication awareness will have negative impacts on credibility and erode trust over time. Before I hit send on any electronic message, I reflect on my objective and consider my audience. Often when I'm experiencing an emotional response, I'll write a message, leave it for a bit, return to it, read it out loud, then decide if I should send it. Nine times out of 10, I'll probably delete it, then pick up the phone or schedule a video chat. Slowing down the action might seem hard at first and counter-intuitive when you are plowing through your to-do list, but it saves you a lot of trouble long term.

Third, you can't win an argument or resolve a conflict using digital tools. Let me repeat that, **never** use digital channels to argue or confront someone. It never, ever ends well. I want you to return to the first paragraph of this section. Digital messages are legally actionable so they can be taken out of context and used against you. Also, if someone has sent you an unprofessional message that feels personal, appreciate that anything you send in response will a) read as defensive, and b) provoke an escalated response. Since digital communication is flat, without tone or affect, it is the emotion of the people involved that color how a message is interpreted. Don't inflame the situation with a response and don't put others in a difficult situation by sending emotional messages. When faced with an uncomfortable situation, don't avoid the issue, or use digital channels. Go "old school." Get offline and schedule time to privately address your concerns.

Reduce Message Distortion by Connecting Directly to Your Audience

When I first started leading remote teams, technology was a lot different than it is today. I recorded messages about important business updates and product rollouts by hiring a video production team to film me reviewing the information, then we took the resulting video, burned a bunch of compact discs (CDs), and sent them to the team through the mail (by mail, I mean the post office) then emailed instructions. Now I can use an internet video platform to talk to one person or a million people all at once and never leave my home office. Last month, I participated in a conference hosted in Moscow. Several of my fellow panelists were live on stage while I arrived virtually from my home in Providence, RI along with a colleague from Baltimore, MD. Our faces were projected on screens at the event, and I even had a real time translator helping me to overcome the language barrier. That's how far things have come, and I have a feeling we've barely gotten started exploring what's possible.

There are so many cost-effective, time efficient ways to bring people together nowadays and while it would have been wonderful to be able to travel to Moscow to attend the event in person and I do personally enjoy face-to-face interactions, it wasn't a cost-effective or practical solution for this event. Yet, even as a virtual guest, I was able to participate in a meaningful way and make contacts that I otherwise would have missed without this virtual option. This is the future of communications. It's flexible, it's hybrid, and it's technically enabled. Anyone can now cost-effectively and time-efficiently produce content, broadcast messages, and connect with individuals or groups via webinars, livestream broadcasts, video chats, pre-recorded messages (audio and video), virtual conference rooms, as well as a thousand other ways. Yes, it's still possible to travel to far away locations and be physically present, but sometimes that doesn't add enough value to justify the time and expense. We need to recognize when in person isn't the best business answer. Technology is so good and so affordable there's no excuse anymore for not offering a virtual option to your remote team members so they can participate in whatever work event you happen to plan.

Taking a flexible approach offers advantages and opens interesting opportunities for company leaders to interact with their teams, their customers, and the public in new and innovative ways. Traditionally, getting a message out to employees and other constituents meant risking the telephone game. You know the one I mean. That's the game when you whisper a message in someone's ear, then have them pass it down through the chain of command and watch it contort into something unrecognizable based on each person's interpretation. Not anymore. In a remote work operating model, a senior leader in a large organization can circumvent traditional hierarchy and control the message directly, creating connection with whomever they choose through their chosen device. We've seen everyone from politicians to CEOs bypass hierarchy and connect with an audience using digital channels, pre-recorded video messages, or livestream, virtual events that connect them directly with an audience of their choosing.

These types of communication forums translate well to any size company and are a great strategic tool for supporting your overall remote team communication plan. For example, during an implementation rollout this type of large group virtual communication forum is a valuable tool when time and resources are limited. Necessary and timely information can be conveyed to a large group with one event. Frequent information updates delivered in a virtual forum with a standard, consistent format that allows for some moderated Q&A can help ease the team's anxiety over a demanding rollout schedule. It helps a remote team feel they aren't in it alone and makes the task seem more doable. As things change rapidly during a rollout, a standing all-hands update meeting can address these changes openly and proactively. Set up a system for collecting questions beforehand so prepared remarks address concerns that are top of mind but leave time at the end for open questions as well. Addressing questions indicates there is nothing to hide. Have a trained moderator help with these events and communicate the rules of engagement to keep things civil and professional.

Virtual and hybrid events can be recorded to create a reference archive for team members unable to attend or for future study. Adding these types of virtual events to your communication plan also allows you to strategically convey information directly to large groups while you and other forum presenters role model the company's remote communication protocols. Well run meetings that convey a positive, calming tone can help ease tensions and build team confidence. Frequent exposure helps executive leaders seem more approachable. When combined thoughtfully with your other communication touchpoints and aligned with your stated goals, mission, and values, these forums can become important for transmitting and reinforcing team culture that can continue to serve an important purpose well beyond your implementation roll out.

Highlights

Leverage the online to offline (O2O2O) communication flow

- Communication flows differently today, rather than a simple, closed loop interaction, communications move fluidly online to offline to online, a phenomenon I call the O2O2O Effect.
- This is how social and digital media works, it keeps us connected constantly, both passively and actively, over time.
- These constant touchpoints can break down natural barriers that exist between strangers as this continual contact breeds familiarity between strangers.

Communication in remote teams works differently

- Face-to-face communication has many contextual non-verbal indicators and even then, misunderstandings occur.
- Remote team communication, dependent on digital tools, internet connectivity, and trust between distant parties, is much more complicated and far more likely to miss the mark.
- Digital communication lacks body language and other contextual cues, they are devoid of tone of voice.
- Digital messages are interpreted and assigned by the recipient based on their state of mind and their relationship (or lack of relationship) with the sender.
- Emojis and emoticons are used to add tone and context to a message but aren't always appropriate in business communications and the symbols mean different things to different people.
- I've provided you with a list of some basic communication rules, but I urge you to invest in remote multi-channel communication training for yourself and your people as it will provide a huge ROI for your business.

Build remote team communication systems then standardize them

- Remote teams need communication protocols and established standards of conduct to prevent chaos and continual misunderstandings.

Create touchpoints that build remote team engagement

- Every element of your remote work operating model is a touch point, adding cultural elements to each element.
- Day in, and day out communications also set a tone and help create the team culture.
- Make sure your touchpoints align with your business goals, mission, and values.
- Touchpoints mold culture, support work efficiency, build trust, and elevate productivity. Don't squander them.

Teach yourself and your people channel etiquette

- There is no standard etiquette for individual digital channels these days. Different people use digital channels differently.
- As the remote team leader, it's up to you to raise this topic with your people.
- Standardize the channels and establish basic etiquette, then invest in training and hold yourself and the team accountable.
- While there are some general rules for how channels work today, this is changing all the time, stay current and make it an expectation that everyone will continue to educate themselves as things continue to evolve.

Recognize digital communication limits

- Digital messages are trackable, traceable, and legally actionable.
- They can be shared easily, taken out of context, and used against you.
- Use of digital speeds up people's response time and that sometimes leads to sending messages before we take time to consider the potential impact or consequences.
- Slow down and refrain from sending until you can review a message with a clear head.
- Never use digital channels to argue or confront someone.
- Go "old school," pick up the phone, schedule a video call, or, if possible, meet in-person.

Reduce message distortion by connecting directly to your audience

■ It used to be harder for senior leaders to connect directly with their people.
■ Traditionally, messages passed through many hands before reaching line employees, causing message distortion as the message passed through many hands.
■ New technology that is widely available, easy to use, and cost effective now allows leaders to circumvent these hierarchies and talk directly with an audience.
■ This is a powerful tool for leaders in any size organization to create virtual or hybrid all-hands forums that can become one additional important remote team engagement touchpoint.

Note

1. This is particularly important if you tend to have a direct communication style like me – I compose my messages, then go back and add my social niceties just before I send the message.

Chapter 12

Institutionalizing Remote Work

Implementations and operationalization are the first step, the real work begins when the implementation winds down, and your operation teams take over to institutionalize the new remote work business model and optimize it. Institutionalizing means the plan is normalized. It moves beyond something new to become the status quo, the way you do business going forward. During the implementation, you embed all the elements into everyone's day-to-day process and your change management work drives adoption. Now you must fully embrace the new model and support and maintain it daily to make sure it aligns with all the new stuff you worked so hard to put in place. The success of this step will be transformative as it is what allows you to achieve the return on investment (ROI) you envisioned at the beginning of this exercise. The elements I cover in this chapter include:

- plan beyond the roll-out
- budget to support the new model
- build business goals tied to remote work
- hire and promote using the new model
- align the performance review process
- track progress, communicate, and report gains

Plan Beyond the Rollout

I've taken you through the planning and implementation steps for adopting a new remote work business model. Planning beyond the rollout is a crucial step that a lot of people forget. Once you are live, don't pull the implementation and

DOI: 10.4324/9781003243557-12

support teams too early but do prepare for an orderly handover. By planning for this, you can ensure the implementation has a recognized completion date with an official handover plan so there is a clear, definite moment when the implementation team steps back, and the operation teams move forward on their own. This allows you to celebrate the implementation team, say thanks to everyone who supported your change efforts. Once these accolades are completed, everything is in place, and things are moving forward nicely, it's easy to think your work is done. It's not. In many ways it's like a marriage, with lots of excitement early on – the romance, the engagement, wedding planning, wedding day, honeymoon. But any married couple knows once the honeymoon is over, that's when the real work begins. The excitement of the rollout ends, and now the day-to-day operational realities begin. This is the final phase of the process where you and your team must institutionalize the new model and learn how to manage it to maximum efficiency.

As this is a new business model, accept there is a shakedown period and a learning curve. It will take time for things to settle to get a true read on profitability, productivity, and other important business success indicators. Choose the operations team carefully – your original pilot groups will be furthest along in the process, keep any eye on them as they are early indicators of wins and potential problems. Handpick your operations teams for these groups – choose people with capabilities whom you trust. Accept this is unfamiliar territory and any historical data from previous models are not a valid comparison. Keep track of data week to week to chart changes and rely on your operations teams most familiar with the processes to evaluate business efficiencies gained. You have to pay attention to the week to week, month to month comparisons of the new model to stay on top of things. Year over year comparisons to old data are not relevant or helpful. Avoid the temptation to compare the old model and the new model for at least a year. The only time old metrics are useful evaluation tools is when the old metrics are still valid against the new model. This must be a true fit, not wishful thinking. Comparisons of this nature that are forced or misaligned will create real problems for you and undercut all your hard work. Be honest about this and don't take shortcuts as anyone with influence who harbors a grudge or who hates the change will seize on any opportunity to declare the new model the culprit given the chance.

I once worked with a highly successful regional retail company that launched a new brand completely different from the existing operations. The company was over 60 years old, and a significant percentage of the company's older executives opposed this new venture initiated by a new, younger president. But the older executives got outvoted. As the first two remote operations opened for business, the older executives and their operation leaders kept comparing the new operating model to their old operating model because that's all they knew.

They used old reporting structures and metric comparisons month after month to point out perceived operational deficiencies. This slowed the momentum of the new operations as it distracted focus and made it hard for the new teams to advocate for needed resources. This distraction allowed the dissenters to persuasively claim the new venture a failure month after month. Calls for shedding the new brand got loud quickly and the new brand leaders, always on the defensive, got distracted fighting off criticism rather than focusing on the new model's operational gains and new market share potential.

Advocates of the new brand never prepared for the disconnect and those that opposed the new brand quickly took control of the narrative. The new brand leaders failed to prepare everyone in advance for the need to evaluate against a new measurement framework. Then they failed to offer an alternate narrative or provide a compelling business case for making the shift to a new set of metric indicators early in the planning and implementation process. Instead, they wasted time and resources trying to shout down the dissenters. Unsurprisingly, because data was different, and the measurement framework was faulty, key stakeholders and executive decision makers were persuaded the new brand's poor business results indicated the brand was unsound. Even though it was unfair to compare the new model to the old one – it was comparing apples to oranges – no one with influence intervened on the new brand's behalf. As a result, the new model never received a true evaluation on its own merit and within 18 months, the company shut down the new brand just as it was finding its footing. The overall loss to the company was in the millions.

You won't have good comparison data for a while. Because there is a shakedown period and a team learning curve, appreciate the first couple of fiscal quarters are not the time to fully judge performance. Rather, track progress to your business targets like you track work performance with your remote employees – incrementally. Day to day to start, then week to week, month to month and quarter to quarter. Don't get too aggressive for the first 12 months, be realistic and adjust your expectations as is appropriate.

Budget to Support the New Model

Just as you need metrics and reporting that reflect the new structure for accurate business analysis and business decision making, you also need new budget models. Every operating structure will have unique financial variables that could significantly impact your operating costs, often for the better. When you adopt a remote work operating model, an obvious example is workspace. A dear friend of mine who owns a digital marketing firm just found this out when he made a dramatic decision in 2021 to sell his office building and take his company virtual after his entire team worked from home successfully for two full years. This was a major sea change for my friend as he and I had engaged in lively debates about remote work for years. Despite much prompting, he always insisted his team needed the office environment for business and cultural reasons to stay productive and motivated. Fast forward to the end of 2021 and things have changed. Now he acknowledges how glad he is to be free of the stress of owning business real estate as he reaps the benefits of remote teams, a larger labor pool for specialized talent, reduced overhead, and improved profit margins. Other budget areas that could be affected by a shift to remote work include:

- IT – support, helpdesk, and devices
- Third party vendors for remote networks, security, cloud applications, and work platforms
- Employee compensation and benefits
- Business liability insurance and other insurance needs
- Fixed costs – utilities, taxes, etc.
- Services like building maintenance, cleaning, ground maintenance, etc.
- Supplies for breakrooms, cafeterias, etc.
- Paper supplies, printer supplies, office supplies, etc.
- Professional development, training, employee recognition, incentives, etc.

There will be more areas unique to your circumstance. Anticipate this in advance, use the pilot groups to start tracking things early so you can work with your finance folks to build an initial budget template that gets you started and helps you to prepare your leadership team and the operators for the shift as the rollout advances and is fully operationalized. Since you have invested a lot in building your remote work business model, do pay close attention to this step. Don't cut corners. It takes 30 days to break a habit and much longer to make new ones. You need at least one or two revenue cycles before you can begin to get a handle on things. By keeping close to things, you can remind your team of this and continue to positively control the narrative.

Build Business Goals Tied Directly to Remote Work

Institutionalizing your new remote work operating model requires all your activities and business efforts to align together in a seamless way. Setting business goals thoughtfully, even when there are many unknowns, help you prepare your team for the shifts and keep your implementation narrative proactively on the offensive. What gets measured gets done. By embedding company business goals into all aspects of your business planning process – your strategic plan, your yearly business goals, and other elements of your business operations, they become behavioral drivers that send the message this is how we're doing business now and how work performance will be judged. It signals the company is all in and helps managers and supervisors accept the change and explain it to their skeptical team members. The first step is tying the change permanently to the other institutional indicators mentioned in this chapter.

Hire and Promote Using the New Model

All the work you did retooling the new hire candidate profiles, new hire recruiting process, hiring, onboarding, and training means new hires won't see your new model as new. For any new employee, what you teach them is just the way things get done. As you adjust your hiring to align with the new competency models, job requirements, and skill attributes, then new employees joining the team will adapt quickly and set a pace that will challenge existing employees. However, there is an inherent tender period after the handover when new employees coming into your organization will be faced with existing managers, supervisors, colleagues, and co-workers who may work hard to impose old habits. This is when your choice of new hire trainers will pay off. Prep new hires during this period so they understand the company is in transition and prepare them for a certain amount of resistance from existing employees. Give them the support they need to meet these challenges.

Your existing employees are experiencing the change differently than your new hires. All the retooling to your talent management process comes to life here as you institutionalize the Leader-Led Accountability Model, embedding the new leadership principles into your professional development programs, and evaluating performance against your new systems. Nothing speaks louder than consistent recognition for adoption of and adherence to the new systems. This includes identifying top talent and awarding choice assignments and promotions to remote employees who excel within the new model using the new remote work criteria. Once ambitious existing employees see this tangible evidence that the way forward is to jump onboard with remote work, they will take advantage and use the new model to try to move themselves ahead.

If there are employees who simply can't make the change, be prepared to let them go. This is important. Keeping destructive personalities too long will disrupt adoption and damage morale. I'm a firm believer in giving everyone a fair chance and making sure they have every opportunity to succeed, but not everyone will make it. Accept you can't save everyone, and you will have to terminate those hardcore dissenters to fully institutionalize the change. Sadly, sometimes terminating a toxic personality for just cause achieves positive results as it signals your commitment to your new plan and indicates to existing employees you are willing to make the hard calls for those unable or unwilling to adapt. It shows support and respect for compliant team members, your early adopters, and all new hires. Few people enjoy terminating employees as it's an unpleasant and emotional task. Use the accountability cycle to give the employee every chance. But stay resolute and committed to the long-term success of the team. Stay on top of this and act early rather than waiting as these situations rarely resolve themselves amicably and can quickly become difficult and toxic.

In Chapter 11, I discussed the importance of communicating thoughtfully during your implementation. It's important that open, transparent communication continues during this phase as well. Keep the narrative positive and forward focused on your end vision. Put plans in place to celebrate, highlight, and elevate these early success stories because these institutional stories will become part of the company lore your teams will tell about getting ahead. Newsletters, key promotional announcements, livestream town halls with open Q&A opportunities, verbal acknowledgement of top performance in public settings, balanced accountability feedback sessions, performance review summary discussions, as well as professional development plans for individual employees expressing an interest in advancing their career are all examples of touchpoints that can reinforce the new model.

Align the Performance Review Process

Once you tie change to performance reviews and someone's pay, it gets people's full attention. If remote work adoption is tied to business goal setting, the Leader-Led Accountability Cycle, the performance review system, promotions, and compensation, employees immediately take notice. It's another validator and adds institutional integrity to your new remote work model as it ties remote work capabilities to someone's path to compensation, career advancement, and possible promotion.

Track Progress, Communicate, and Report Gains

This is a continuation of your communication strategy using business metrics and your new reporting structure to demonstrate business results. You want to codify your new reporting structure. When data fuels the narrative, you have useful validation. Be honest and transparent with your business results – good and bad. Verbalize the progress to goal at all levels so there is less doubt things are working. If something is amiss, then this proactive approach gives you time to consult with your team, identify the root cause of the problem then present the plan for fixing it so the team understands the path forward. You started your drip campaign a long time ago in the initial stages of your planning process, controlled the messaging and the story during your rollout. Keep it up through this phase as well until remote work is a part of your company's DNA, fundamental to its brand and corporate identity.

Highlights

Plan beyond the rollout

- Build a plan for a clear handoff that indicates the rollout is complete and the new model is now the way you do business.
- Stay in control of the narrative so dissenters aren't allowed to introduce negativity at the early stages of the handover.
- Prep your leadership team for things in advance and rely on your implementation team to take over operations as they know the new systems the best.
- Build your metrics day by day, week by week, and month by month.
- Use your new reporting structure and the results of the pilot as guidelines as they are a more accurate reflection of the new remote work operating model.
- Avoid using old metrics and outdated business metrics to evaluate the company's progress against goals.

Budget to support the new model

- Just as you need the new metrics and reports to evaluate the business, you also need new budget templates adjusted to the new operational realities of your new remote work operational structure.

Build business goals tied directly to remote work

- Business goals beyond the rollout need to support and institutionalize your new remote work operating model.
- Ensure the goals align with the systems, processes, and structure you implemented in your rollout, so it institutionalizes the change.

Hire and promote using the new model

- Fully leverage the talent management systems you implemented in your rollout so new hires reflect the remote work competencies, job skills, and functional capabilities.
- New hires will get pressure from some existing employees to return to the old ways.
- Prepare your new hires for this and hand pick your new hire trainers to ensure they provide support and reinforcement of the new systems.
- Identify existing employees who adopt and adhere to the new systems for choice assignments and promotions to indicate all the new criteria you intend to use to support career growth.
- Give every employee an opportunity to succeed but accept you can't save everyone.
- Deal with dissenters using the Leader-Led Accountability Cycle and terminate those unable or unwilling to adopt and adhere to the new structure.
- Address problems early to avoid operational disruptions before events become toxic and disruptive.

Align the performance review process

- Align your promotion, professional development, business goals, and career paths to the new remote work operating model.
- When performance reviews and career advancement are tied to employee compensation, employees take notice.

Track progress, communicate, and report gains

- Plan for continuing to communicate company performance and business progress toward goals beyond the handover.
- Data builds institutional integrity when it is balanced, transparent, and honest.
- Proactively use data to identify root cause problems, consult your team for solutions, and present your mitigation plans to keep the team focused on problem solving and positive future growth.

Chapter 13

Build on Team Achievements

Congratulations for making it this far! You have much to celebrate. Once your remote team is working effectively, don't get complacent. Continue to provide meaningful, business-oriented challenges by getting your remote teams deeply involved with root cause problem solving when operational issues present themselves. Use this as an opportunity to continue to strengthen engagement, build team resilience, and help your people maintain an open-minded approach toward change. Do this by continually acting as a role model.

- recognize achievements, become a spokesperson
- keep iterating
- up the ante over time

Recognize Achievements, Become a Spokesperson

Congratulations! You put in the work and your new remote work operating model is yielding results. Keep up the momentum by celebrating your success with your people as well as the business community at large. Do this inside and outside your company. Address your professional organizations, networking groups, or offer yourself as a panelist for vendor events. Transformations like this should not be kept secret. Become a role model example for the rest of the world. There are lots of ways to do this now – podcasts, conferences, webinars, industry events…become the one everyone turns to as an example of success. It's one of the reasons you did this – to elevate your brand. It's a great selling tool to build new revenue opportunities, launch new services, introduce new products

DOI: 10.4324/9781003243557-13

or lines of business, and potentially penetrate new markets. If you aren't currently a public speaker, it's time to become one, update your LinkedIn profile, publish an article on your implementation journey, tell your story and celebrate the work. During your rollout, keep a journal documenting your experiences and make this the basis for your narrative. Speak on behalf of your company and your star performers. Speak on behalf of those who collaborated with you or have them represent the team or the company themselves, so they get exposure and recognition for their contributions.

Keep Iterating

As part of your ongoing strategy, prepare to continually evaluate and modify as you gather data that helps you evaluate your business progress against your plan. Business today is not a build-it-and-forget-it, one-and-done situation. Everything we've discussed in this handbook is continually dynamic and fluid. Any business wishing to remain competitive must continue to evolve and adapt as the world continues to redefine how work gets done going forward. Today it's video conferencing, tomorrow it will be virtual reality, augmented reality, and artificial intelligence. Keep learning and challenge your people to do the same. If you invest in remote work now, you have a chance to shape the future of the workplace. I challenge you to help us refine universal remote work standards by sharing your experiences and your lessons learned. Recognize you are part of a business shift that is not yet fully defined. I invite you to contact me through our Sophaya or Remote Nation Institute websites and tell me your story so we can share your experiences with your fellow remote work community members.

Up the Ante Over Time

Professional development isn't a luxury, it's a necessity to maintain business vitality and sustain growth. Once you build a dynamic learning organization, remote employees get restless if they don't see opportunities to continue to grow. Support your employee's curiosity and challenge them by maintaining your company investment in professional development and proactively creating on the job opportunities for remote employees to continually stretch their skills. Learning helps all of us stay current and relevant in a world of constant change. The beauty of the Leader-Led Accountability Cycle is its emphasis on continual community growth. At the end of each accountability cycle, work collaboratively with your employees to identify new avenues of development and growth that suit the employee's interests and contribute to your company's future.

Don't neglect your own development. As remote team leadership models continue to transform and modern technology becomes cost effective, stay ahead of your competition by continuing to try new things. Since remote work models are based on adoption and retooling to accommodate change, keeping you and the team on their toes – whether you are one day on the job or 10+ years on the job – helps sustain the organizational resilience needed to continue to transform as the world evolves. Stay on the lookout for new opportunities as you and your team continue to grow.

Highlights

Recognize achievements, become a spokesperson

- Once your remote work model is in place, use your implementation story to elevate your brand and create visibility for your company.
- Become a public speaker inside and outside your company to spread the word.
- There are lots of opportunities these days – industry events, panels, podcasts, webinars, vendor events.

Keep iterating

- Stay on top of your game by continuing to challenge yourself and your team.
- Remote employees who stay curious and challenged are more resilient and adaptable.
- Today it's video conferencing, tomorrow it's virtual reality, augmented reality, and artificial intelligence – stay open to what's next.
- Contact me at Sophaya or the Remote Nation Institute and share your story with our remote work community.

Up the ante over time

- Build a learning organization that is ready to transform itself by staying curious and growing its capabilities.
- Investments in professional development are necessary as professional development fuels team resilience.
- Don't forget to invest in your own development so you can continue to lead your remote team through transformation in the future.

THE END!

Bibliography

Derek Sivers: How to start a movement. https://www.ted.com/talks/derek_sivers_how_
to_start_a_movement

Kübler-Ross E. and Kessler D. (2014). *On Grief & Grieving: Finding the Meaning of
Grief Through the Five Stages of Loss.* New York: Scribner. ISBN 978-1476775555.
OCLC 863077888

Kübler-Ross E. (1969). *On Death and Dying.* New York : The Macmillan Company.
ISBN 0026050609

Index

Note: Page references in *italics* indicate figures.

Printed in the United States
by Baker & Taylor Publisher Services